The Existence of God
and the Faith-Instinct

The Existence of God
and the Faith-Instinct

Howard P. Kainz

Selinsgrove: Susquehanna University Press

Associated University Presses
2010 Eastpark Boulevard
Cranbury, NJ 08512

The paper used in this publication meets the requirements of the American National Standard for Permanence of Paper for Printed Library Materials Z39.48-1984.

Library of Congress Cataloging-in-Publication Data

Kainz, Howard P.
    The existence of God and the faith-instinct / Howard P. Kainz.
       p. cm.
    Includes bibliographical references (p.) and index.
    ISBN 978-1-57591-143-4 (alk. paper)
    1. God (Christianity) 2. Faith. I. Title.
    BT103.K35   2010
    231'.042—dc22

                                                    2010012061

PRINTED IN THE UNITED STATES OF AMERICA

For my grandchildren

Contents

Preface

Books against religion and belief in God are plentiful in our day and often make the best-seller lists. Witness the success of Richard Dawkins's *The God Illusion,* Christopher Hitchens's *God is Not Great,* Daniel Dennett's *Breaking the Spell,* and Sam Harris's *Letters to a Christian Nation.* But a particular handicap of such books, and of atheism in general, is that it is impossible to prove the *non*-existence of *any* being, in the universe as a whole. Realizing this, Richard Dawkins, to his credit, "hedges his bet," admitting that his certainty about God's *non*-existence is only a 6 on a scale of 7.[1]

The success of such would-be exposés indicates that a lot of people are interested in finding out more about the non-existence of this particular being. Considering this ongoing negative interest, how then are we to make sense of St. Paul's assertion, when speaking against "those who suppress the truth," that "What can be known about God is evident. . . . Ever since the creation of the world, his invisible attributes of eternal power and divinity have been able to be understood and perceived in what he has made. As a result, they have no excuse."[2] "*Evident,*" says St. Paul! He speaks as if it should be straightforward for any rational and open-minded person to come to a belief in the existence and power of a divine Being. But, as a matter of fact, there was relatively little atheism in that era, compared to our own, although theism took on many forms, often idolatrous and superstitious, and even cruel.

What is it in our era that keeps us from making what St. Paul considered to be the obvious deductions about God, and then go on from there? If being surrounded by God's creations—that is, natural things—is an important factor in recognizing the Creator, this seems to be lacking in the modern industrialized world. In ancient times,

1. Richard Dawkins, *The God Delusion* (New York: Houghton Mifflin, 2006), 51.
2. Rom 1:19–20. *New American Bible,* 1993–94, used for all biblical citations.

11

even in cities and towns, there was an admixture of natural objects and human creations; stars could be seen at night, and the cycles of the seasons were an unmistakable environment for all. We denizens of the twenty-first century, even in rural areas, where the stars might still be visible, are often surrounded by technological creations for transportation and communication and convenience. Even the effects of the elements are blocked with climate-control devices. In other words, many of us are surrounded almost exclusively by human creations. If we would look for reflections of the Creator, about the only available resource might be other human beings—many of whom might be just as obsessed with man-made creations as we are, and in some of whom the image of God in which humans are allegedly made[3] has been obscured, voluntarily or by detrimental influences from others.

Another factor hindering our movement in the direction St. Paul indicates may be a heady enthusiasm for the empirical sciences, which has affected the modern world since the eighteenth-century Enlightenment. The feeling is in the air that all the answers to our questions about the world are at hand, if we just patiently adhere to the scientific method; and it is even supposed that a practical directedness of life, producing maximum happiness for all, will be the inevitable result of mushrooming developments in science and technology.

The "downside," however, is that science can deal effectively only with material things, and the most reliable conclusions of empirical science are quantitative or mathematical. If "things" like God and values and the meaning of life are not material, and not susceptible to quantitative measurements, science can only arrive at the *borders* of certain questions, but cannot proceed any further.

A long-standing, and almost traditional, obstacle to belief in the existence of God has been the existence of evils in the world: How could a good God allow such an unending and unwelcome series of cataclysms of nature, debilitating physical conditions, and ruthless atrocities produced by evil men? In fact, the last item—the inhumanity of humans to fellow humans, *homo homini lupus*—is perhaps the major obstacle to any belief that we are created "in the image of God." The enormous weight of this "inhumanity-problem" is not unconnected to the progress of technology—a side effect of which has been the potentiating of the weapons of war, which now can produce levels of de-

---

3. Gn 1:26–27; 9:6.

struction that were absolutely unimaginable in previous eras. We learn about gas chambers into which unwanted groups have been driven and "neatly" exterminated; weapons of mass destruction beyond the wildest dreams of vengeance of even the most insane demagogue; and even a "doomsday" scenario, in which the explosion of nuclear warheads could set off environmental reactions leading to a "nuclear winter," killing off all life above the level of a grasshopper.

In chapter 2, such exemplifications of the "problem of evil" will receive special treatment, after consideration of the evidence of God's existence. Then, hopefully, the way will be paved for discussion, in chapter 3, of God's characteristics, to see if the lineaments of God can be ascertained more concretely.

In the final four chapters of this book, various aspects of faith will be considered. Faith itself is an issue surrounded in the contemporary world with difficulties equally as formidable as those encountered with regard to the question of God's existence. In St. Paul's time, the first Christians encountered many other claimants for their faith besides the Jewish religion that provided the cultural environment for many of them; and formidable divisions emerged—some considered "heretical"—among the Christians themselves. But this ancient divisiveness seems negligible compared to the present situation, in which hundreds of denominations exist among Christians themselves, some of them considering all others as heretical, or even diabolical. The direction of faith is uncertain: "If the bugle gives an indistinct sound, who will get ready for battle?"[4] For those who look to the Bible as a major source for their faith, the fact that so many parts of the Bible are called into question by historical-critical scriptural scholarship presents problems. For Roman Catholics who look to the Petrine rock of authority for leadership, difficulties in faith arise when influential theologians call into question the authority of the Vatican, especially in regard to moral issues. In addition, Eastern religions are making headway in the Western world, along with strange pseudoreligions like Scientology and New Ageism. This is not to mention that science itself has become a total belief system, and indeed a way of life, for some.

In the midst of so many contemporary claimants, my intention in this book is to engage in a basic reconsideration of faith, with a view to elucidating the Christian faith, and also its relation to faith outside

4. 1 Cor 14:8.

the parameters of Christianity. I begin in chapter 4 by considering the fact that the concept of faith in the New Testament seems to go well beyond both traditional Catholic *and* traditional Protestant under-standings of the meaning of faith. In chapter 5, with the help of an extensive commentary by the German theologian, Max Seckler, I focus on St. Thomas Aquinas's theory that faith is an instinctive en-dowment in all rational beings. (If this is true, all the efforts of dedi-cated atheists to remove religion, once and for all, may be doomed to failure. And "faith in atheism," as a quasi-transcendent goal, may be just one more possible misdirection of the basic faith-instinct, for some individuals.)

In chapter 6, following up on the theory of the faith-instinct, I con-sider the problem of what would, and should, be the "proper objects" of this basic human faculty. Finally, in chapter 7, taking the lead from Seckler's treatment of the *Nichtevangelizierten,* I take up the question concerning the operation of faith, and the attainment of salvation, outside the parameters of the evangelized Christian world, and es-pecially in vast areas of the world where evangelization is impossible.

Some excellent books have appeared recently, combating the "New Atheism" of Dawkins and others. These include Berlinski's *The Devil's Delusion,* Hahn and Wiker's *Answering the New Atheism,* Vox Day's *The Irrational Atheist,* Feser's *The Last Superstition: A Refutation of the New Atheism,* Novak's *No One Sees God,* Ganssle's *A Reasonable God,* Craig and Meister's anthology, *God is Great, God is Good,* and Hart's *Atheist Delusions.* My purpose in this book is not to add additional refutations of the New Atheists, but rather to reexamine the "God-question," theodicy, and the various meanings and manifestations of faith. The movement in this book is from the general to the particular. The process of development of faith that I describe is the sort of scenario in which one step (for example, belief in God's existence) might lead logically to a following step (for example, considering the compati-bility of God with the realities of evil in the world), and this would lead to the following step—questions concerning the characteristics of God and the meaning of faith—and end with a consideration of ecumenical issues in a world of multiple, and often contradictory, re-ligious faiths. Although the distinctive path individuals take to and through faith will vary, seeing the logical progression here described may be conducive to an understanding of the twists and turns, or dead ends, factored into one's own faith journey.

The Existence of God
and the Faith-Instinct

1

The Existence of God

Anyone who approaches God must believe that he exists, and that he rewards those who seek him.

—Hebrews 11:6

PHILOSOPHERS ARE NOTORIOUS FOR RAISING ESOTERIC QUESTIONS THAT would hardly occur to most people. One of the most esoteric questions still under consideration has to do with the existence of an external world. Ancient philosophers such as Pyrrho and Sextus Empiricus raised questions about our knowledge of an external world, and modern philosophers like Descartes, Malebranche, Berkeley, and Mill placed such heavy emphasis on subjective thoughts, feelings, or sensations that certainty about external reality was discountenanced. Descartes, for example, suggested that our experience of the external world could be produced by the trickery of some demon, and Berkeley, taking a more sanguine view of the possibilities, concluded that our apprehension of an external world is produced directly by God or spirits, so that we receive perceptions spiritually produced, but still have no certainty of direct sensory contact with things outside of our own perceptions. Some contemporary epistemologists still take this problem seriously, raising questions about the objective correspondences of our perceptions. How do we know, for example, that we are not dreaming rather than awake? And if we are in a waking state, how can we be sure that we are not experiencing illusions, delusions, or other distortions of reality?

But most people, including most philosophers, are willing to admit, or even accept wholeheartedly, the existence of an external world. Some philosophers who specialize in refuting the arguments of ancient or modern skeptics often point to factors or experiences—like painful molestations from outside—that make sense only if we assume an external world. They also bring up inconsistencies of the

17

skeptics themselves regarding the *un*skeptical way in which they deal with, and act upon, the external world. But many people, less tolerant, will throw up their hands in exasperation and refuse to engage in argument with anyone who takes such an absurd position as to deny external reality.

People of faith will often respond to those who doubt or deny the objects of faith in a similarly exasperated way—like Franz Werfel, who at the beginning of his book, *The Song of Bernadette*, says, "For those who believe, no explanation is necessary; for those who don't believe, no explanation is possible." Werfel was referring to supernatural phenomena associated with the life and work of Bernadette Soubirous in the nineteenth century. Like the defenders of common sense against doubters of an external world, people of faith may think it a fruitless endeavor to try to disabuse doubters of their skepticism.

Søren Kierkegaard goes even further than Werfel, considering any attempt to prove God's existence as insulting:

> Let us mock God, out and out, as has been done before in the world— this is always preferable to the disparaging air of importance with which one would prove God's existence. For to prove the existence of one who is present is the most shameless affront, since it is an attempt to make him ridiculous; but unfortunately people have no inkling of this and for sheer seriousness regard it as a pious undertaking. . . . An omnipresent being can only by a thinker's pious blundering be brought to this ridiculous embarrassment.[1]

In a similar vein, theologian Karl Barth argues that for someone with faith in God to actually step back and engage in arguments about God's *existence* would be demeaning and insulting to some interlocutor to whom only rational arguments are addressed, and would only obfuscate the reality that is faith: "Not without justice—although misconstruing the friendly intention which perhaps motivates us—he [the interlocutor] will see himself despised and deceived. He will shut himself up and harden himself against the faith which does not speak out frankly, which deserts its own standpoint for the standpoint of unbelief. What use to unbelief is a faith which obviously knows different?" And after an exhaustive dialectical examination of possibilities that a believer could justifiably take the standpoint of the unbeliever and utilize arguments from "natural theology," Barth concludes:

---

1. Søren Kierkegaard, *Concluding Unscientific Postscript*, trans. David Swenson (Princeton: Princeton University Press, 1941), 485.

A theology which seeks another knowability of God is incontestably impossible in the sphere of the Church; incontestably, because from the very outset a theology of this kind looks in another direction than where God has placed himself, and therefore involves, from the very outset, a violation of the Christian concept of God.[2]

One can only admire the conviction and certainty of the faith expressed by Kierkegaard or Werfel or Barth. But their observations about the irrelevance of any proof of God's existence are only half-truths. True, there is a simple faith that needs no explanations, and true, there are unbelievers whose mind-set is impervious to faith. But, as Alvin Plantinga points out, even those for whom faith in God qualifies as a "properly basic" belief, grounding all sorts of beliefs and actions, can justifiably engage in apologetics. They are eminently rational when they address potential or actual "defeaters" of this belief (for example, the problem of evil brought up as disproof of a good God), hopefully to "defeat the defeaters."[3] Thus theologians can quite commendably busy themselves with clarifying beliefs that may be insufficiently understood, or misunderstood; and philosophers can commendably try to remove some of the obstacles that prevent our intellects from opening up to other dimensions, and from taking what Kierkegaard called the "leap of faith." On the other hand, we should not ignore the formidable problems that arise when it comes to *proving* the *existence* of God.

SPECIAL PROBLEMS IN PROVING THE EXISTENCE OF GOD

An initial problem in proving the existence of *anything*, as pointed out by Thomas Aquinas,[4] is that we have to identify by name that whose existence we are attempting to verify. Thus, if God were a physical being, we could give a physical description, possibly even a very graphic description, which would constitute a "name," and then begin our search. For example, if we identified God-as-physical with the resurrected Jesus, as someone with certain physical qualities within the observable universe, in principle this object of our search would

---

2. Karl Barth, *Church Dogmatics* II, I, 93, 126.

3. Alvin Plantinga, "The Reformed Objection to Natural Theology," in *Rationality in the Calvinian Tradition*, ed. Hart, Van der Hoeven, and Wolterstorff (Lanham, Md.: University Press of America, 1983), 382.

4. *Summa theologiae* I, q. 2, a. 2, ad 2. Hereafter the *Summa* will be abbreviated *S. T.*

be locatable by a space probe with extraordinarily advanced instruments. If God were an idea, possibly an innate idea, we would be able to question someone, and find out if he or she has that idea—just as Socrates in one of Plato's dialogues[5] questioned an uneducated slave boy and, by a series of questions, discovered the existence of the concept of the Pythagorean theorem in the boy's mind. St. Anselm famously suggested we would easily find in most people the idea of God as "the most perfect being, than which nothing greater can be thought" and that this idea, if it was really the "greatest," would imply real existence (which is certainly greater than mere existence-in-thought). But as Aquinas showed,[6] this would be a mistaken idea of perfection, since the undoubted greatness of the *idea* of "real existence" doesn't necessarily *produce* real existence.

God is frequently identified as the "first cause," but we should realize that this is an anomalous and paradoxical way of speaking, since every cause that we are familiar with is in a linear series of causes, being the effect of some other temporally preceding cause, and temporally preceding its own particular effects. God would certainly not be imbedded in any such line of causality. Thus, if God were a cause, He would be an *uncaused* cause, the cause of all the concatenations of causes in the universe, the cause of causation itself—in other words, not a "cause" in any of our usual meanings of the word.

Aquinas suggests[7] that our initial identification of God should be through His effects. And *de facto* some of the "names" that are given to God have to do with His effects: "creator," "supreme lawgiver," "redeemer," etc. The investigation of God's existence through effects leads, not surprisingly, to "Scotland Yard" approaches to proof: the philosophical investigator searches for clues that show the vestiges of some extraordinary, superhuman power or intelligence responsible for the effects in question. Like a detective, he may go through various putative "suspects," comparing them in terms of their explanatory power, and finally concluding with the best possible explanation.

This "Scotland Yard" approach would seem to jibe well with the methodologies of physics and cosmology—leading some scientists to search for evidence, in the macrocosm or the microcosm, of developments that seem to bypass nature and physical laws. But this type

---

5. See the *Meno*, 82–85.
6. *S. T.* I, q. 2, a. 1, ad 2.
7. *S. T.* I, q. 2, a. 2, ad 2.

of investigation has a downside: Any clues that are discovered will be mathematical or numerical, in accord with the specific methodologies of empirical science. The result may be the discovery of extraordinary statistical improbabilities, and the God that results would be a phenomenal supercomputing mathematical mind—not exactly what many people are looking for in God. But perhaps this is a beginning that can lead eventually to a more comprehensive depiction.

COSMOLOGICAL ARGUMENTS

In a 1948 debate between Father Frederick Copleston and philosopher Bertrand Russell concerning the existence of God Father Copleston began by focusing on the question of the origin of the cosmos and the need for a "First Cause." After a considerable amount of give-and-take on this issue, Russell simply indicated that he did not see any significance to the question, saying, "I do think the notion of the world having an explanation is a mistake. I don't see why one should expect it to have. . . . [The scientist] does not assume that everything has a cause. . . . What do you say—shall we pass on to some other issue?"[8] Father Copleston agreed to this suggestion and moved on to proofs based on ethical and religious experience. But since that time, the situation has changed considerably. Indeed, in recent decades, physicists seem to have been the most prominent in exploring scientific grounds for theistic belief. One physicist has remarked, "If we need an *atheist* for a debate, I go to the philosophy department. The physics department isn't much use."[9] Hugh Ross offers us an extensive list of respected physicists and cosmologists who view the fine-tuning of the universe as proof of a Designer.[10] Even the late Fred Hoyle, longtime proponent of the steady state theory of an eternal uncreated universe, and an inveterate atheist, complained that a "superintellect has monkeyed with physics, as well as chemistry and biology."[11] And physicist Paul Davies, unable to avoid crossing the boundary line between physics and metaphysics, observes:

8. Bertrand Russell, *Why I Am Not a Christian* (New York: Routledge Classics, 2004), 137–38.

9. Robert Griffiths, mathematical physicist, quoted in Tim Stafford, "Cease-Fire in the Laboratory," *Christianity Today*, April 3, 1987, 18.

10. See Hugh Ross, *The Creator and the Cosmos* (Colorado Springs: Navpress, 2001), 157–60; and *Creation as Science* (Navpress, 2006), 50–51, 96–97.

11. See Hoyle's "The Universe: Past and Present Reflections," *Annual Reviews of Astronomy and Astrophysics*, 20 (1982), p. 16.

The very fact that the universe *is* creative, and that the laws have permitted complex structures to emerge and develop to the point of consciousness—in other words, that the universe has organized its own self-awareness—is for me powerful evidence that there is "something going on" behind it all. The impression of design is overwhelming. Science may explain all the processes whereby the universe evolves its own destiny, but that still leaves room for there to be a meaning behind existence.[12]

The type of evidence that is continually brought to the fore from such physicists has to do with the completely unexplainable exact formation after the "big bang" of particles, elements, forces, galaxies, stars, and planets, and the precise proportion of "dark" matter and energy to "ordinary" matter and energy—all that is needed to give rise to a galaxy and solar system able to produce the sort of carbon-based life that is featured on our planet. Physicist-theologian Stanley Jaki sums up some of the evidence as follows:

If gravity had been stronger by one part in 10^{40}, the universe would have long ago undergone a catastrophic collapse instead of a systematic expansion. Again, if the strength of the initial explosion, or Big Bang, had been different by one part in 10^{60}, the universe would have taken on a very different evolutionary course. . . . If [the ratio of the combined masses of proton and electron to the mass of the neutron] had been slightly less, hydrogen atoms would become unstable and the sun would have long ago faded. Again a slightly different ratio of the respective strengths of the electromagnetic and nuclear forces would prevent the formation in supernovae of that very element carbon, which is the mainstay of organic life as we know it. Further, a mere five percent decrease in the strength of nuclear force would prevent the formation of deuterium which has a key role in the nuclear chain reaction within the sun and makes it possible for the sun to become a stable, long-lived star. As to neutrinos, the lightest of all fundamental particles, if their mass had been ten times larger than their actual value, or 10^{-34} kg, they would have, because of their very large number, caused a gravitational collapse of the universe.[13]

In other words, the most infinitesimal shift in such junctures in the evolution of the universe would have rendered the whole life-production enterprise impossible. The infinitesimal mathematical "probabil-

    12. Paul Davies, *The Cosmic Blueprint: New Discoveries in Nature's Creative Ability to Order the Universe* (New York: Simon and Schuster, 1988), 203.
    13. Stanley Jaki, *The Purpose of It All* (Washington, D.C.: Regnery Gateway, 1990), 101–2.

ities" that are listed by some physicists—sometimes with the numerator as a "one" over a hundred zeros in the denominator—merge conceptually with *impossibility*, unless some sort of design, in which all the laws and forces of nature are coordinated purposefully, is envisioned.

ARGUMENTS FROM BIOLOGICAL EVOLUTION

"Intelligent Design" (ID) is currently one approach to proving the existence of a supranatural intelligence through examination of the evolution of species. The ID movement was sparked during the 1980s through two books by scientists challenging some tenets of Darwinian theory: *Evolution: A Theory in Crisis,* by Michael Denton[14] and *The Mystery of Life's Origin: Reassessing Current Theories,* by Charles Thaxton, Walter Bradley, and Roger Olsen.[15] Both books threw doubt on the received wisdom concerning naturalistic/materialistic explanations of evolution and revived inevitable questions about the possibility of a supernatural being directing evolution, or at least intervening at certain stages. Proponents of ID often refrain from using the designation "God," but the Intelligent Designer that they specify has all the earmarks of the deity.

This approach is contrasted with, and opposed to, the mainstream neo-Darwinian theory of "natural selection," which is an interpretation of the development of the species by processes of random mutations in specific environments leading to "survival of the fittest," and which hypothesizes that the variations taking place within species also produced transitional forms leading to completely new species.

Proponents of ID generally accept the fact that there has been a gradual evolution of biological species (microevolution), but they also focus on missing "branches" in the "tree of evolution," and especially on the almost total lack of evidence for leaps from one species to another (macroevolution). They challenge neo-Darwinists to explain the sudden appearance in biological evolution of complex organisms whose complexity cannot be reduced to multiple prior developments through "natural selection." For example, in the Cambrian era of evolution (505 to 570 million years ago), all sorts of aquatic and other creatures appeared, for which no transitional fossils have been found.

14. Bethesda, Md.: Adler & Adler, 1986.
15. New York: Philosophical Library, 1984.

Similar unexplained gaps seem to prevail in the transition from hominids to *Homo sapiens* (about 150,000 years ago)—not to mention the emergence of the first cellular organisms from inorganic matter billions of years ago, for which there could be *no* transitional living fossils.[16] David Berlinski, referring to biologist Eugene Koonin's "big bang" model of biological evolution, sums up the sorts of cases that cannot be explained by the Darwinian theory of gradual transitions from one species to another:

> [According to Koonin,] "major transitions in biological evolution show the same pattern of *sudden emergence of diverse forms at a new level of complexity.*" Major transitions in biological evolution? These are precisely the transitions that Darwin's theory was intended to explain. . . . Facts that fall outside the margins of Darwin's theory include "the origin of complex RNA molecules and protein folds; major groups of viruses; archaea and bacteria, and the principal lineages within each of the prokaryotic domains; eukaryotic supergroups; and animal phyla." That is, pretty much everything.[17]

Darwin himself seems to have left an opening for an alternative to natural-selection types of explanation when he remarked, "If it could be demonstrated that any complex organ existed which could not possibly have been formed by numerous, successive, slight modifications, my theory would absolutely break down."[18] This remark needs some further analysis. If Darwin had actually *proven* empirically that some complex organ *had* been formed by "numerous, successive, slight modifications," this would be a generous concession. But he did not. In lieu of proof, he was merely theorizing, "This is the way complex organs are formed, and I challenge doubters to show that my theory will not work"—in other words, putting the burden of proof on the doubters. Nevertheless, some ID theorists, instead of relying on the logical maxim, *quod gratis asseritur, gratis negatur* ("what is gratuitously affirmed can be gratuitously denied") have actually tried to address this challenge. Thus Michael Behe points to organs, such as the flagellum of the E. coli bacterium, which are "irreducibly com-

16. See, for example, William Dembski, ed., *Mere Creation: Science, Faith & Intelligent Design* (Downers Grove, Il.: InterVarsity Press, 1998).

17. David Berlinski, *The Devil's Delusion: Atheism and Its Scientific Pretensions* (New York: Crown Forum, 2008), 192–93.

18. *Works of Charles Darwin*, ed. Paul H. Barrett and R. B. Freeman, vol. 16, *The Origin of Species*, 1876 (Charlottesville, Va.: Intelex Corporation, 2001), 154.

plex," insofar as multiple parts operate like a machine in which the removal of any one part would disable the organ. He argues that such organs could not have been produced by gradual evolution over millennia, adding parts incrementally.[19] Also, regarding Darwin's sanguine belief in gradual complexification, Behe extrapolates from the *known* progress of mutations in rapidly reproducing organisms such as mosquitos, and calculates that the change from pre-chimp ancestors to *Homo sapiens* would have taken longer than the age of the universe.[20]

But how can we know for certain that various modes of "natural selection" could *not* have produced such results? How can we know that all possible avenues of change have been examined? Imaginative neo-Darwinians have countered with arguments concerning algorithms for "fitness functions" and "target sequences" that might have taken place gradually over millions of years. Aside from the question of the validity of arguments that employ algorithms,[21] it must be conceded even by ID proponents that there is no way of *scientifically* demonstrating the *negative* of Darwin's assertion; there is no possibility of ruling out from consideration the trillions of mutations that *might* have taken place over billions of years.

Philosophers of science often point out the characteristic of a true scientific theory as being "falsifiable"—that is, offering some possibility through experiment or observation of showing that the theory doesn't work. This criterion is relevant to certain areas of science—for example, if a chemist predicts that a certain reaction will take place under certain conditions, leaving open the possibility that his peers might be able to create the same conditions to see if the reaction takes place or not. But it is undeniably difficult to imagine a way of *scientifically* demonstrating the *negative* of Darwin's observation that "the number of intermediary and transitional links, between all

19. See Michael Behe, *Darwin's Black Box: The Biochemical Challenge to Evolution* (New York: Free Press, 1996).

20. Michael Behe, *The Edge of Evolution: The Search for the Limits of Darwinism* (New York: Free Press, 2007).

21. See William A. Dembski, "Why Evolutionary Algorithms Cannot Generate Specified Complexity," *Metanews* (1999): Nov. 1, 1999, (www.discovery.org/a/10). "Evolutionary algorithms . . . can yield specified complexity only if such algorithms along with their fitness functions are carefully adapted to the complex specified targets they are meant to attain. In other words, all the specified complexity we get out of an evolutionary algorithm has first to be put into the construction of the evolutionary algorithm and into the fitness function that guides the algorithm. Evolutionary algorithms therefore do not generate or create specified complexity, but merely harness already existing specified complexity. Like a bump under a rug, the specified complexity problem has been shifted around, but it has not been eliminated. . . ."

living and extinct species, must have been inconceivably great"[22]—
which implies (contrary to the situation up to the present) that many,
or at least a few, of such transitional links would be found! Who could
falsify this statement? Who can be sure that the links will not eventually turn up? Stanley Jaki points out the difficulty of dealing with the
innumerable lacunae of such links in any scientifically commendable
fashion:

> Today with the number of known living and defunct species being of the
> order of six million, those [transitional] links should have existed in the
> billions. None of them have yet turned up. This remains so in spite of
> Stephen J. Gould who greeted the discovery, in a seabed in Pakistan, of
> the fossil named *ambulocetus natans* (swimming-walking whale), as "the
> sweetest series of transitional fossils an evolutionist could ever hope to
> find." Anyone with moderate expertise in what constitutes a "series"
> would take for wishful thinking Gould's statement that the discovery was
> "a remarkable smoking gun."[23]

The announcement of the discovery of "Tiktaalik," said to be a "missing link" between fishes and land animals, and promoted in the *New
York Times* as a rebuttal to the "creationists,"[24] and followed up more
recently in the *Times* with publicity about the discovery of the mon-
key-like "Darwinius masillae" (nicknamed "Ida") as a possible link to
humans,[25] might inspire a similar question as to where is the "series"?
On the other hand, how can one rule out the remote possibility that in
some future paleontological expeditions, thousands of such links will
begin to emerge?

However, *even if* thousands of transitional forms began to show up
in paleontological digs to fill the missing gaps, what would this prove?
Not that there is no purpose behind the abstraction of "natural selection," but the opposite. David Stove, who describes himself as being "of no religion," but concerned about the excesses of Darwinism,
uses an analogy of artificial selection carried out by humans on plants
or animals to point out that "natural selection" *implies a purpose:*

22. Darwin, *Works, Origin,* 278.
23. Stanley Jaki, *Questions on Science and Religion* (Port Huron, Mich.: Real View Books, 2004),
119.
24. See "Fossil Called Missing Link from Sea to Land Animals," *New York Times,* April 6, 2006.
25. Ibid., "Seeking a Missing Link, and a Mass Audience," May 18, 2009.

[Richard] Dawkins . . . writes . . . "Natural selection . . . has no purpose in mind. It has no mind and no mind's eye. It does not plan for the future. It has no vision, no foresight, no sight at all." These statements, (though excessively repetitive), are all true. But alas, they are trivial. For they would still all be true, if we were to put for their subject, instead of "natural selection," "artificial selection." Artificial selection has no purpose in mind. (Cattle breeders have, though.) Artificial selection has no mind. It does not plan for the future, (though wheat geneticists do). But no one would be tempted to infer, from these truisms, that purposeful intelligent agents play no part in bringing about *artificial* selection![26]

Special Significance of DNA in Current Debates

In December 2004, the famous atheist philosopher, Antony Flew, announced that, taking into account scientific discoveries, and reexamining his former arguments, he could no longer remain an atheist, but had "willingly suspended belief" in atheism.[27] Flew notes that in making this move he is joining a formidable group of twentieth-century scientists—Einstein, Heisenberg, Schrödinger, Planck, and Dirac.[28] Flew's most important incentive for changing his mind to "something like" the deism of Thomas Jefferson and Einstein was the "unbelievable complexity" of the DNA programming that led to the evolution of life. In 2004, when asked if research on the origin of life points to a creative intelligence, he replied:

Yes, I now think it does . . . almost entirely because of the DNA investigations. What I think the DNA material has done is that it has shown, by the almost unbelievable complexity of the arrangements which are needed to produce (life), that intelligence must have been involved in getting these extraordinarily diverse elements to work together. The enormous complexity of the number of elements and the enormous subtlety of the ways they work together. The meeting of these two parts at the right time by chance is simply minute. It is all a matter of the enormous complexity

26. David Stove, *Darwinian Fairytales* (Brookfield, Vt.: Avebury/Ashgate, 1995), 186

27. James A. Beverley, "Thinking Straighter: Why the World's Most Famous Atheist Now Believes in God," *Christianity Today*, April 2005, 80–83. In line with his new perspective, Flew provided a new introduction to the 2005 reprinting of his *God and Philosophy* (Amherst, N.Y.: Prometheus Books, 2005), and the changes in Flew's position are discussed by Paul Kurtz in the Publisher's Foreword to that edition.

28. Antony Flew, with Roy Abraham Varghese, *There Is a God: How the World's Most Notorious Atheist Changed His Mind* (New York: Harper One, 2007), 103–6.

by which the results were achieved, which looked to me like the work of intelligence.[29]

Similar considerations constituted a major step on the way that led Francis Collins, director of the Genome Project, from atheism to Christianity.[30]

Indeed, the genetic instructions that constitute the core of all life development seem to defy scientific explanation. Cornell geneticist J. C. Sanford, after examining all the proposed theoretical scenarios in which mutations might be an integral element of evolution through "natural selection," focuses on the genome:

> What is the mystery of the genome? Its very existence is its mystery. Information and complexity which surpass human understanding are programmed into a space smaller than an invisible speck of dust. Mutation/ selection cannot even begin to explain this.[31]

Stephen Meyer, following up on Bill Gates's comment that "DNA is like a computer program but far, far more advanced than any software ever created,"[32] offers an extended analogy of the informational properties of the genome to computer operating systems and programming,[33] and concludes:

> The Genome and the cell's information-processing and storage system manifest many features—hierarchical filing, nested coding of information, context dependence of lower-level informational modules, sophisticated strategies for increasing storage density—that we would expect to find if they had been intelligently designed.[34]

In tandem with such reflections, recent approaches in ID theory focus not on "missing links" in the evolutionary "tree," or the "irreducible complexity" of certain organs, but on the "specified complexity" of the DNA instructions, which operate like a computer program in producing the functional proteins that are responsible for all the vari-

29. Ibid., 75.
30. See Francis Collins, *The Language of God: A Scientist Presents Evidence for Belief* (New York: Free Press, 2006), 199.
31. J. C. Sanford, *Genetic Entropy & the Mystery of the Genome* (Lima, N.Y.: Elim Publishing, 2005), 151.
32. *The Road Ahead* (New York: Viking, 1996), 188.
33. *Signature in the Cell* (New York: Harper One, 2009), 465 ff.
34. Ibid., 477.

ations in species. These instructions can't be generated by simple rules or algorithms, and thus are "complex" like the words produced by humans from the letters of the alphabet; and they are directly associated with the production of distinct species, and thus are "specified." Stephen Meyer argues that the improbability of such massive production of specified complexity by DNA is so great that the numerical expression of the improbability would have more zeroes than the number of molecules in the universe.[35] And Michael Denton, after proposing as an analogy the impossibility of any program that would show the best move in a game of checkers by testing all possible moves and countermoves,[36] observes

> The Darwinian claim that all the adaptive design of nature has resulted from a random search, a mechanism unable to find the best solution in a game of checkers, is one of the most daring claims in the history of science. But it is also one of the least substantiated. No evolutionary biologist has ever produced any quantitative proof that the designs of nature are in fact within the reach of chance. . . . It is surely a little premature to claim that random processes could have assembled mosquitoes and elephants [as Richard Dawkins claimed in a 1982 article] when we still have to determine the actual probability of the discovery by chance of one single functional protein molecule![37]

Denton concludes that the well-known Darwinian "tree of life" branching out into all the known species through macroevolution can be best understood in a cultural context as a change-resistant element of biological *mythology*.

Nevertheless, it should be realized that neo-Darwinian natural selection happens to be the "reigning paradigm" in the science of biology (even though macroevolution is widely disbelieved by the public at large).[38] As Thomas Kuhn has pointed out,[39] false or inadequate scientific paradigms do not disappear until they are displaced by bet-

---

35. See Stephen C. Meyer, "Intelligent Design: the Origin of Biological Information and the Higher Taxonomic Categories," *Proceedings of the Biological Society of Washington* 117, no. 2, 2004, 213–39; and "DNA and Other Designs," *First Things* 102, April 2000, 30–38. See also *Signature in the Cell*, 212, regarding the improbability of getting functional proteins by chance from an original "prebiotic soup."

36. *Evolution: A Theory in Crisis*, 313–14.

37. Ibid., 324.

38. *The Devil's Delusion*, 186.

39. Thomas Kuhn, *The Structure of Scientific Revolutions* (Chicago: University of Chicago Press, 1970), 77.

ter scientific explanations. Darwin produced evidence that change takes place *within* species through "natural selection" and theorized that the production of new species can be explained through the same process. Do ID theorists have a "better explanation"?

Stephen Meyer maintains that the informational content of the DNA "program" does offer that "better explanation." DNA has all the earmarks of intelligent design, and is presupposed in the processes of natural selection, but cannot itself have been produced by any process of natural selection. Meyer even argues that ID theory made the prediction in 1998 that the so-called "junk" DNA, then thought by most biologists to be products of random events, would turn out to have important biological functions, if it was intelligently designed, and that this prediction has been confirmed in recent years.[40] Meyer offers this as an example of valid scientific predictions that have been made by ID theory, and adds numerous other ID-engendered predictions, which he claims are susceptible to confirmation or refutation by the scientific community.[41]

But whether or not the arguments for intelligent design do have sufficient credentials to provide the "best *scientific* explanation," they do have *philosophical* credentials for those for whom philosophical soundness is a relevant consideration. Indeed, the investigation of evidence for design and purposefulness, as contrasted with chance and randomness, has been a concern of philosophers from time immemorial. At this point we are confronted directly with the philosophical question that has been lurking in the background, while neo-Darwinists argue for the hegemony of chance developments, and proponents of ID counter with probabilistic arguments for evidence of design: aside from arguable mathematical calculations, cannot the human mind attain any certainty about *purposefulness* in nature, or the lack of such purposefulness?

PHILOSOPHICAL ANALYSIS OF THE ISSUES

In the midst of cosmological speculations about the origin of the universe and the evolution of the species, important metaphysical issues arise that are often ignored. In cosmology, the problem of "infinite regress" needs to be considered; and in evolution, the problem of the meaning of "chance" is crucial to the concept of "natural selection."

40. *Signature in the Cell*, 407.
41. Ibid., 497.

The Infinity Problem in Cosmology

As mentioned above with regard to the evolution of the cosmos, the vast amount of evidence that seems to indicate a "fine-tuning" of the universe has led many to look for an explanation through a supreme intelligence, variously conceived. David Berlinski reminisces about the unexpected and (to some) unwelcome dovetailing of the big bang theory with traditional theological explanations, and the consequent attempt of some physicists to overcome the tension caused by this confluence. The big bang sounds suspiciously like creation. So how do physicists avoid the *prima facie* similarity of the big bang theory to Judeo-Christian explanations from Genesis? According to Berlinski, subsequent attempts to explain the theory without any such theological resemblances often involved recourse to highly speculative explanations based on presuppositions of infinities.[42]

Thus some theorists have conjectured that there are an infinite number of universes, or an infinitely massive "mother universe" of which our own universe is just a minuscule part. In the midst of such infinity, they argue, *everything* must have happened, somehow, somewhere, and at some time—so we should not be surprised at the way our particular universe has managed to produce life and consciousness by chance. Like the winners of a lottery, we have just been extremely lucky. In an actual infinity of universes with an actual infinity of facts and events, everything has happened an infinite number of times. Our universe, including its laws, was inevitable amidst an infinite number of chance developments. Problem solved!

But as Paul Davies points out, this conjecture explains nothing:

> It is trivially true that, in an infinite universe, anything that can happen will happen. But this catch-all explanation of a particular feature of the universe is really no explanation at all. We should like to understand the bio-friendliness of this universe. To postulate that all possible universes exist does not advance our understanding at all. Like a blunderbuss, it explains everything and nothing. By contrast, a true scientific explanation would be analogous to a single well-targeted bullet.[43]

And there are other problems. As Michael Behe observes, such an infinity would place us beyond all probability in a never-never land of nightmarish proportions:

42. *The Devil's Delusion*, 81.
43. Paul Davies, "Universes Galore: Where Will It All End?" http://aca.mq.edu.au/Paul-Davies/publications/chapters/Universes%20galore.pdf, 8.

In an infinite multiverse, probabilities don't matter. Any event that isn't strictly impossible will occur an infinite number of times. So (if thinking depends solely on a physical brain), by utter chance in an otherwise dead universe, matter might spontaneously arrange itself into a brain that would contain the true thought, "I am a spontaneously materialized brain in an otherwise dead universe." That will happen a limitless number of times in an infinite multiverse. Matter may also arrange itself into brains with any of an infinite number of false-but-detailed thoughts and memories. . . . An infinite number of universes would harbor an infinite number of "freak observers"—[making all possible observations, some veridical and some illusory.][44]

In other words, all hope of contact with reality as we understand it would have to be given up. Even the physical laws that we depend on could change at any instance, and "laws of thought" would be a euphemism for the chance developments that work their way through our brain and nervous systems.

Davies adds that, ironically, such theories, formulated to make God unnecessary, end up bringing God into the picture:

Consider the most general multiverse theories . . ., where even laws are abandoned and anything at all can happen. At least some of these universes will feature miraculous events—water turning into wine, etc. They will also contain thoroughly convincing religious experiences, such as direct revelation of a transcendent being. It follows that a general multiverse set must contain a subset that conforms to traditional religious notions of God and design.[45]

The fundamental problem with such conjectures is that they presuppose an *actual physical infinity*—material events and entities stretching back in space and time without end. But as Aristotle argued, an infinity of this sort is always *potential,* and can never be actual. In space and time, we arrive at the idea of infinity by considering all finite numbers or measurements we are aware of, and saying that something can be added to them; or by saying that all the divisions we make are subject to further division. In other words, every length of space or time can *potentially* be added to, *ad infinitum;* and every division of space or time can *potentially* be further divided up, *ad infinitum.*

---

44. Michael Behe, *The Edge of Evolution* (New York: Free Press, 2007), 225.
45. "Universes Galore," 10.

Many other philosophers have pointed out the conceptual impossibility of an actual infinity. John Locke observes that the idea of an actual infinity converts something that is essentially a step-by-step process into a *fait accompli* realized once and for all:

> To have actually in the mind the idea of space infinite, is to suppose the mind already passed over, and actually to have a view of *all* those repeated ideas of space which an *endless* repetition can never totally represent to it; which carries in it a plain contradiction.[46]

Immanuel Kant, in his famous *antinomies,* makes a similar point: If there were an infinite time, we wouldn't be situated at some specific point of time, but time would have already passed through an infinite number of points; and our thinking about an infinite space would require us to go through that impossible infinity of moments of time just to conceptualize it.[47] (Kant also argues in the opposite direction —that a finite space and time are impossible. But his reason for this is that whatever limit we arrive at, there are always potential units of space or time that can be added to it *ad infinitum.* That is, a *potential infinity* hovers over every idea of limits, a *beyond* that stands as an additional element ready to be added.)

There are, of course, some ways that geometers can talk about "infinite space," and mathematicians considering abstract theories of classes can refer to "actual infinities." And Stephen Hawking suggested the big bang singularity could be completely avoided by the substitution of imaginary numbers for real numbers, so that the "beginning" of time could be formulated as a smooth curve rather than the point of a cone.[48] But, outside the realm of geometry, pure mathematics, and imaginary numbers—that is, physically speaking—the space of the universe that contains real objects that can be distinguished from one another, and numbered, is always finite. (In mathematical physics, infinities can occur in formulas, but much of the progress of modern physics has consisted of doing away with the need for such infinities. Paul Davies refers to them as "mathematical headaches" that always lead nowhere. He points out that, in recent decades, progress in overcoming infinities has been made by the theory of electromagnetism and gauge symmetry. He sees the at-

---

46. John Locke, *Concerning Human Understanding,* bk. 2, chap. 17, §7.
47. Immanuel Kant, *Critique of Pure Reason,* A427–B455.
48. Berlinski, 101–2.

tempts of physicists to work out a grand unified theory as further progress against infinities. An ultimate challenge is gravity, which is still "plagued with the infinity problem.")[49]

Fantasy aside, the concept of a finite universe has received solid support in the twentieth century from Einstein's theory of relativity, in combination with empirical discoveries confirming the "big bang" theory, which presupposes an expanding universe beginning with a "singularity."

The Problem of "Chance" in Evolution

The belief in chance as the ultimate explanation for life is not of recent vintage, but was a concern even in the Bible:

> The wicked . . . said among themselves, thinking not aright: Brief and troublous is our lifetime. . . . Haphazard were we born, and hereafter we shall be as though we had not been; because the breath in our nostrils is a smoke and reason is a spark at the beating of our hearts.[50]

And Cicero in his *De natura deorum* mentions with bafflement some ancient philosophers who ascribe the development of the cosmos to chance:

> Must I not marvel that there should be anyone who can persuade himself that there are certain solid and indivisible particles of matter borne along by the force of gravity, and that the fortuitous collision of those particles produces this elaborate and beautiful world? I cannot understand why he who considers it possible for this to have occurred should not also think that, if a countless number of copies of the one-and-twenty letters of the alphabet, made of gold or what you will, were thrown together into some receptacle and then shaken out on to the ground, it would be possible that they should produce the *Annals* of [the poet] Ennius, all ready for the reader.[51]

In neo-Darwinism, chance becomes the scientifically respectable explanation for biological progress. The upward path of biological evolution is characterized as taking place through "natural selection," entailing massive amounts of beneficial mutations leading to

---

49. Paul Davies, *God and the New Physics* (New York: Simon and Schuster, 1983), 155–67.
50. Ws 2:2.
51. Cicero, *De natura deorum*, II, 37.

the survival of the "fittest" species. But evolutionists seem to give short shrift to the known fact that the mutations that contemporary biologists are familiar with are generally deleterious or neutral. As Geoffrey Simmons points out:

> Darwinists . . . ignore the scientific facts that [mutations] are exceedingly rare and are either damaging or insignificant. One science writer compared the effect of mutations to that of a shotgun fired at a book. They only make the book harder to read. In contrast, the sharpshooter type of mutation, only picking off a letter or two, will usually go unnoticed and disappear.[52]

Indeed, one may have to conjecture an almost *infinite* process of beneficial mutations leading on the upward path from molecules and microorganisms up to mammals and humans:

> Every aspect of our inner self is managed by billions of DNA compounds and several layers of hundreds of millions of proteins within each cell that somehow know how to do, when to do, and where to do their work. Most actions happen in millionths of a second, but there are some that follow very specific building plans over days, years, and even decades. If . . . we came about through evolution, meaning mere chance, there would have had to have been a near-infinite number of ministeps over unfathomable lengths of time. If life truly began 3.5 billion years ago, it's not likely it would have proceeded beyond mold. And that would only be if everything went right."[53]

It should be noted that such comments about chance developments in evolution constitute a reappearance of the problem of an "actual infinity," just discussed, but transported from cosmology to biology—now, seemingly an actual infinity of favorable mutations providing successful survival for millions of species.

But an even more fundamental metaphysical problem than "actual infinity" occurs in Darwinism. This is because the Darwinian process of natural selection through "chance developments" in organisms and their environments is often referred to as if it were the *cause* of biological evolution. Chance, however, can *never* be a cause of anything.

"Stochastic causality" is sometimes cited as a counterinstance to this rule, since it utilizes certain laws of probability to predict events

---

52. *Billions of Missing Links* (Eugene, Oreg.: Harvest House, 2007), 259.
53. Ibid., 271.

in quantum physics, chemistry, actuarial sciences, meteorology, etc. But chance, by definition, is outside of *any* laws, including laws of probability. As has been noted by Spinoza, Hume, Russell, and other philosophers, what happens by "chance" is simply an event or effect for which *we don't know the cause*. Since such things appear to be random, we might speak loosely about "developments caused by chance." But this is completely inaccurate and misleading. Darwin himself made clear in a number of places that the chance developments he hypothesized in nature were not "causes." For example, he says:

> I have hitherto sometimes spoken as if the variations so common and multiform in organic beings under domestication, and in a lesser degree in those in a state of nature had been due to chance. This, of course, is a wholly incorrect expression, but it serves to acknowledge plainly our ignorance of the cause of each particular variation.[54]

Darwin is even more cautious concerning "blind chance" developments in the production of the *human* species:

> The birth of the species and of the individual are equally parts of that grand sequence of events, which our minds refuse to accept as the result of blind chance. The understanding revolts at such a conclusion, whether or not we are able to believe that every slight variation of structure, the union of each pair in marriage, the dissemination of each seed, and other such events, have all been ordained for some special purpose.[55]

And in his autobiography, he mentions his oscillation between agnosticism and theism, resulting from his doubts about the validity of chance explanations:

> [Reason tells me of the] extreme difficulty or rather impossibility of conceiving this immense and wonderful universe, including man with his capability of looking far backwards and far into futurity, as the result of blind chance or necessity. When thus reflecting I feel compelled to look to a First Cause having an intelligent mind in some degree analogous to that of man; and I deserve to be called a Theist.[56]

---

54. Darwin, *Works, Origin,* 112.

55. Darwin, *Works, The Descent of Man and Selection in Relation to Sex; Second Edition,* Vol. 22, pt. 3, chap. 21, "General Summary and Conclusion."

56. Charles Darwin, *The Autobiography of Charles Darwin* 1809–1882. With original omissions restored. Edited with appendix and notes by his granddaughter, Nora Barlow. (London: Collins, 1958), 92–93.

But for us, as well as Darwin, developments at times do *seem* to be caused by chance. And this phenomenon needs further analysis.

Aristotle in his *Physics* explains the mechanisms according to which chance *seems* to operate as a cause:[57] For example, a man may go out with the purpose of collecting money for a banquet from certain sources, and end up at somebody's house for some other reason (for example, gossip) and then because of favorable circumstances (the presence of an interested contributor), combined with spontaneous reflection, be able to collect money there. This would be "chance" in a positive sense—that is as good luck. If, after his gossip session, he was robbed on the way home, this would be chance in a negative sense —that is, bad luck. In both cases, the notion of chance would be related to the purpose he had in mind. In other words, chance, far from being purposeless, is always related to human purposes. Strictly speaking, "what is not capable of action cannot do anything by chance. Thus an inanimate thing or a beast or a child cannot do anything by chance, because it is incapable of choice; nor can good fortune or ill fortune be ascribed to them, except metaphorically."[58] As applied to nature, the anomalies and quirks and exceptions that we *seem* to witness are not the result of chance, but simply evidence of the fact that nature is purposeful, in the sense that it acts in certain ways "for the most part."[59] Thus we might look metaphorically on a monstrosity as something not intended by nature, and on the production of a genius as something that goes beyond what we would ordinarily expect from nature. We might look upon events in nature as fortunate or unfortunate "chance" events for us, in view of our *own* purposes.

So also, when we in the twenty-first century speak of "innumerable chance developments" that have led to the development of the human species and/or of the universe, this is tantamount to referring to them as exceptions to the laws of physics (laws that don't show any particular propensity for rising to organic complexities and consciousness), and indeed as lucky or fortunate developments (unless we have a Schopenhauerian pessimism about the whole shebang). This psychological process is illustrated in contemporary physics by the "anthropic principle," which views the universe in terms of the

57. Aristotle, *Physics* II, 5, 197a, 5 ff.
58. Ibid., 6, 197b, 6.
59. Ibid., 8, 198b, 36; 199b, 24, 32.

processes that made possible the evolution of carbon-based life.[60] The "weak" version of the anthropic principle simply indicates that, epistemologically, we tend to interpret the evolution of the universe in this way; the "strong" version sees the universe as in some sense *made* for us—at least in the sense that we can't seriously visualize any other kind of universe.

In sum, if we needed to make a Pascalian wager between Chance (with upper-case significance) or God as the cause of the universe, a rational bettor, realizing that "chance" is meaningful only as unexpected developments in the unfolding of physical laws, and that chance cannot, strictly speaking, *cause* anything, would not favor Chance. As Frank Tipler observes, "To accept chance as an ultimate is to accept human ignorance as an ultimate."[61] The human mind, willy-nilly, is constituted to look for causes; but to say that our species has been caused by multiple chance mutations is an abdication of reason, equivalent to saying vacuously that it has been caused by multiple "I-know-not-whats."

Of course, as mentioned above,[62] there are also considerable difficulties with the notion of God as "cause"—since God characterized as Cause of the whole series of causes in the universe would not be a cause in any of the usual ways that we use the term "cause." But if our rational bettor was able to accept a paradoxical *uncaused* cause—needed to terminate an otherwise unexplainable series of causes and effects—he might be willing to favor God as the obvious "default" choice over Chance.

SUBJECTIVE APPROACHES TO GOD'S EXISTENCE

Medieval philosophers influenced by the Aristotelian concept of teleology often cited the principle, "Nature does not do anything in vain" (*natura non agit frustra*), and often applied this principle to questions about natural desires. Aquinas, for example, regarding the question about whether angels could have a limited lifetime, argues that angels, as intellectual creatures like us, would be able to apprehend perpetual existence as a good and desire it, and this natural desire could

---

60. See John D. Barrow and Frank J. Tipler, *The Anthropic Cosmological Principle* (Oxford: Oxford University Press, 1986).

61. Frank Tipler, *The Physics of Christianity* (New York: Doubleday, 2007), 130.

62. See p. 20.

not be in vain.[63] Similarly, with regard to a question about whether the passion of anger (*ira*) was useful or not, he concludes that it is useful for helping humans to achieve their rational goals (especially difficult goals)—otherwise "this sensory appetite would exist in man in vain, since nature does nothing in vain."[64] This principle does not, of course, apply to every desire, but to desires or appetites fundamentally connected with human nature—that is, being a rational animal. The desires for self-preservation, propagation of the race, knowledge of the truth, and orderly social arrangements would be further examples of desires that are purposefully implanted in humans.[65] Most relevant to our present examination, Aquinas takes the natural desire for the beatific vision of God in the afterlife as an inclination that "would be inane" if not fulfilled.[66]

The presence of a natural desire, of course, does not guarantee that one will actually attain the object of that desire. If, as Aristotle notes,[67] all humans have a natural desire for happiness, this does not ensure that they will attain it. It only ensures that everyone, even a masochist or a person who commits suicide, will be pursuing happiness directly or indirectly, positively or negatively, in the actions they carry out.

St. Augustine in a prayer supposes that there is a similar inevitability in the desire for God:

> We humans, who are a due part of your creation, long to praise you—we who carry our mortality about with us, carry the evidence of our sin and with it the proof that you thwart the proud. Yet these humans, due part of your creation as they are, still do long to praise you. You arouse us so that praising you may bring us joy, because you have made us and drawn us to yourself, and our heart is unquiet until it rests in you.[68]

Augustine, taking his own meandering autobiographical paths as evidence, predicts psychological distress if one tries to ignore, or find substitutes for, this natural desire. One is reminded of St. Paul's "goad" that he was apparently opposing or ignoring before his conversion

---

63. Aquinas, *Summa contra gentiles* II, 55.

64. ("alioquin, frustra esset in homine appetitus sensitivus, cum tamen natura nihil faciat frustra"), Aquinas, *S. T.* II-II, q. 158, a. 8, ad 2.

65. Aquinas, *S. T.* I-II, q. 94, a. 2c.

66. Aquinas, *S. T.* I, 1. 12, a. 1c.

67. Aristotle, *Nichomachean Ethics*, bk. 1.

68. Augustine, *Confessions*, trans. Maria Boulding (New York: Vintage, 1998), I, 1.

("it is hard for you to kick against the goad").[69] According to Augustine, the result of this existential situation, for someone who has caught sight of the goal, is intense spiritual discomfort:

> Woe betide the soul which supposes it will find something better if it forsakes you! Toss and turn as we may, now on our back, now side, now belly —our bed is hard at every point, for you alone are our rest.[70]

A similar, Augustinian path to recognition of God's existence is described by the twentieth-century Spanish philosopher, Unamuno:

> As I sank deeper and deeper into rational scepticism on the one hand and into heart's despair on the other, the hunger for God awoke within me, and the suffocation of spirit made me feel the want of God, and with the want of Him, His reality. And I wished that there might be a God, that God might exist. And God does not exist, but rather super-exists, and He is sustaining our existence, existing us. . . . This Supreme Consciousness . . . This God, the living God, your God, our God, is in me, is in you, lives in us, and we live and move and have our being in Him. And He is in us by virtue of the hunger, the longing, which we have for Him, He is Himself creating the longing for Himself. . . . God is in each one of us in the measure in which each one feels Him and loves Him. . . . The true God is He to whom man truly prays and whom man truly desires.[71]

Unamuno is aware of the problem posed above—that a natural desire does not necessarily guarantee attainment of the desired object. His solution hinges on the fact that the "object of desire," in this special case, is *within* us. The longing for God is, as it were, the necessary, but not sufficient, springboard for finding God. In order to actually find God, some diligence is required:

> Not to believe that there is a God or to believe that there is not a God, is one thing; to resign oneself to there not being a God is another thing, and it is a terrible and inhuman thing; but not to wish that there be a God exceeds every other moral monstrosity; although, as a matter of fact, those who deny God deny Him because of their despair at not finding Him.[72]

On the other hand, many people *are* apparently able to arrive at the conviction of the non-existence of God without undergoing the

69. Acts 26:14.
70. *Confessions*, VI, 26.
71. Miguel de Unamuno, *Tragic Sense of Life* (New York: Dover Publications, 1954), 169, 177.
72. Ibid., 184.

deep personal anguish chronicled by Augustine and Unamuno. The philosopher Jean-Paul Sartre (1905–80) was committed to developing a sound, unassailable atheistic philosophy. According to Simone de Beauvoir, Sartre complained once that "all the great philosophers have been believers more or less. That means different things at different times. Spinoza's belief in God is not the same as Descartes' or Kant's, but it seemed to me that a great atheist-, truly atheist-philosophy, was something philosophy lacked. And it was in this direction that one should now endeavor to work."[73] Consistent with this firm intent, Sartre, who maintained that the concept of God is incompatible with freedom, mentions in his autobiography that he only once had a concrete experience of the presence of God, and boasts that he resolutely rejected this experience, and was never bothered with it again.[74]

But whether a subjective or an objective approach is taken, if the God whose existence is being investigated is the Judeo-Christian God, a seeker would be well advised to turn to the Scriptures, where a clue is offered as to what sort of existence might be ascertained.

USING REVELATION AS AN AID

God as *existence*

As mentioned above,[75] Aquinas emphasizes that the starting point for asking about the existence of anything or anyone is to specify the object of the search by name. Thus a doubter who is trying to determine whether or not God exists might do well initially to specify as precisely as possible the object of his investigation, before proceeding to questions of existence. With an open mind, he may even look to the Bible for an indication of identity. There is one place in the Old Testament that can be interpreted as a quest for the proper identification of God. In Exodus 3:14, Moses, after being commissioned by God to lead the Israelites out of Egypt into the Promised Land, mentions to God that, if the Israelites should inquire about his credentials as a prophet, he should be able to identify who it is that is sending him. God seemingly obliges by answering, in Hebrew, *ehyeh*

---

73. Simone de Beauvoir, *Adieux: A Farewell to Sartre* (New York: Pantheon, 1984), 436.

74. Jean-Paul Sartre, *The Words*, trans. Bernard Frechtman, (New York: Braziller, 1964), 102.

75. See above, 19.

asher ehyeh, translated in the Greek Septuagint as *ego eimi ho on,* and in the Latin Vulgate as *ego sum qui sum.*

Down through the centuries, there has been considerable debate among scholars in many languages, regarding even the best literal translation of these words, not to mention the meaning of the original Hebrew words after they have been literally rendered. The late Jewish Bible scholar, Nahum Sarna, presents three possible literal translations of *ehyeh asher ehyeh* in his commentary on the Jewish Publication Society's Torah. These are: "I Am That I Am"; "I Am Who I Am"; and "I Will Be What I Will Be."[76] Unfortunately, in English, expressions like these, taken at face value, could be interpreted as dismissive or even insulting. But this is obviously not the case in the context of Moses's encounter with God. Moses is a messenger who, to be heeded by the Israelites, requires clear evidence of his authorization.

A literal English translation of the Greek Septuagint's rendition, given above, could be "I am the Existing," and the Latin Vulgate rendition could be translated into English as "I am the one who is." Current English translations of this phrase in Exodus 3:14 now vary from "I am that I am" (King James Version) to "I am who am" (Douay-Rheims and New American) to "I am who I am" (Jerusalem Bible and World English Bible).

But this diversity of opinion is only relevant to the first part of verse 14, where God is identifying Himself to Moses. More unanimity prevails with regard to the latter part of the same verse, where the Hebrew term *ehyeh* is used for a third time, and God tells Moses to identify himself to the Israelites as "*ehyeh.*" Almost all English versions translate this as "I am"; the Vulgate and the Douay-Rheims as "he who is." Thus Moses goes to the Israelites and tells them he has been sent by "I am." This "I am" then, Hebrew scholars tell us, becomes incorporated etymologically into the term, "Yahweh," as the name of God, repeated over six thousand times in the Old Testament (but translated in English versions ordinarily as "the Lord"). Thus, to paraphrase, a Hebrew in saying "Yahweh" would be meaning something like "the One who exists," with an emphasis on the personal aspect entailed by the first-person singular, "I am."

Someone with Platonic or Plotinian tendencies might see these renditions as the theological counterpart to the philosophical idea of

---

76. See *Exodus, The Traditional Hebrew Text with the New JPS Translation,* Commentary by Nahum Sarna (New York: Jewish Publication Society, 1991), 17, n. 13.

"existence itself" (*auto to einai*), and it would be an understatement to say that both Jewish and Christian philosophers have found the text of Exodus 3:14 intriguing. The medieval Jewish philosopher Moses Maimonides interprets the passage as a divine call to the Israelites to recognize God as "the existing Being which is the existing Being"—that is to say, the Being whose existence is absolute,[77] and Aquinas observes:

> God is existence itself, and so when Moses inquires (Exodus 3:14) what God's name is, the Lord responds, "I am He who exists."[78]

The above passage, and relevant passages from Exodus, could also be translated ". . . who is" instead of ". . . who exists." But since, in English, statements in the form "x is . . ." usually end up with a predicate specifying and limiting the subject, "exists" seems a preferable translation. In English, if a statement like "I am" or "He is" is encountered, the common reaction would be "I am what"? or "He is what"? "I exist" would not elicit such questions.

Most important, if "Yahweh" in the Hebrew Bible, as the name of God repeated over and over again, connoted something like "He who exists," Maimonides and Aquinas and others would seem to be justified in perceiving the metaphysical implications of this usage, although the biblical authors were not metaphysicians. For if God is existence itself (or Himself?), does it make sense to ask, tautologically, whether existence exists?

In other words, there is an initial paradoxical ambiguity about the subject of this sentence. Stones and dollar bills and people exist, but in each case to say that it exists delimits the subject to some particular type. Even corpses exist, as corpses. If we consider whether existence exists, it is clear we are dealing with an anomalous subject, which resists delimitation, and which is not a "subject" of a sentence in any usual sense.

There is also an ambiguity about the predicate of the sentence. The act of "existing" is ordinarily used as a lowest common denominator inferior to more advanced and interesting activations. For example, we might speak dismissively concerning a building, observing that the

---

77. Moses Maimonides, *Guide of the Perplexed,* 2d. ed. pt. 1, chap. 63, trans. M. Friedlander. (New York: Dover Publications, 1956), 95.

78. Thomas Aquinas, *Sancti Thomae Aquinatis Tractatus de Substantiis Separatis,* chap. 17, sect. 93, ed. Francis Lescoe (West Hartford: St. Joseph College, 1962), p. 136.

building "exists," with the implication that it is not being used well, or that it is not architecturally pleasing; and if we were asked about the importance of John or Harriet, we might answer sardonically that they "exist," with the implication that they are not doing much more than that. But in the present case we are referring to existence as the highest possible activity. When "Yahweh" is called upon as "He who exists," the reference is to the core actuality that gives rise to and sustains all actuality. To express the unique usage of "existence" with regard to God, Aquinas uses the analogy of fire, without which no greater or lesser degrees of heat would be possible.[79]

If, then, one means by the name, "God," existence in the fullest sense, the usual questions about the existence of God would not, and could not, occur, unless—going even beyond the esoteric philosophers mentioned above who argue about the existence of an external world—we wish to carry our doubts about *existence itself* to the ultimate extreme.

---

79. *S. T.,* I, 2, a. 3, corpus.

2
The Problem of Evil

Is [God] willing to prevent evil, but not able? then is he impotent.
Is he able, but not willing? then is he malevolent. Is he both able
and willing? whence then is evil?
—David Hume: *Dialogues Concerning Natural Religion*, X

BECAUSE OF OUR EXPERIENCE OF MULTIFARIOUS EVILS IN THE WORLD,
it is possible that one could be intellectually convinced of God's existence, but doubt that He is in reality personally concerned with us
and the world we live in, as the provident and benevolent Father of
all mankind. In Hume's terminology, there is a difference between
the "metaphysical" and the "moral" acceptance of God's existence.
Hume, expressing his ideas through the character, Philo, in his *Dialogues Concerning Natural Religion,* grants to the believer, Cleanthes,
that arguments from design may be convincing, but the idea of God's
goodness falls by the wayside when we consider the evils in the world:

> Here, Cleanthes, I find myself at ease in my argument. Here I triumph.
> Formerly, when we argued concerning the natural attributes of intelli-
> gence and design, I needed all my sceptical and metaphysical subtlety to
> elude your grasp. In many views of the universe and of its parts, particu-
> larly the latter, the beauty and fitness of final causes strike us with such ir-
> resistible force, that all objections appear (what I believe they really are)
> mere cavils and sophisms; nor can we then imagine how it was ever pos-
> sible for us to repose any weight on them. But there is no view of human
> life, or of the condition of mankind, from which, without the greatest vi-
> olence, we can infer the *moral* attributes, or learn that infinite benevo-
> lence, conjoined with infinite power and infinite wisdom, which we must
> discover by the eyes of faith alone.[1]

1. David Hume, *Dialogues Concerning Natural Religion* X, para. 37. Italics added.

This stands as an accurate summation of the position of "deism," which became widespread in the 18th century in Europe and America. It is a view that sees salient evidence of design—at least of a mechanistic sort—in the universe, but indicates we would have to do "violence" to our rational faculties to believe in a good and benevolent God, because of our manifest experience of evils in the world.

François Marie Arouet de Voltaire (1694–1778), a major spokesman for deism, gravitated decisively to deism in response to the great Lisbon earthquake of 1755. The news that reached the rest of Europe described massive destruction and incomprehensible suffering. Possibly ninety thousand people were killed, many in church (since the earthquake took place at the hour for Mass on All Saints day), fires lasted for a week, a tsunami with waves twenty feet high hit Lisbon and other nearby coastal areas. Voltaire responded with a long and impassioned poem expressing revulsion and rejection of all explanations for such evils. He includes in the poem sarcastic remarks about the philosopher Leibniz, who argued in his theodicy that our world is "the best possible world," and about the poet Alexander Pope, who painted a too sanguine picture of the world:

> Come, ye philosophers, who cry, "All's well,"
> And contemplate this ruin of a world.
> Behold these shreds and cinders of your race,
> This child and mother heaped in common wreck,
> These scattered limbs beneath the marble shafts—
> A hundred thousand whom the earth devours,
> Who, torn and bloody, palpitating yet,
> Entombed beneath their hospitable roofs,
> In racking torment end their stricken lives.
> To those expiring murmurs of distress,
> To that appalling spectacle of woe,
> Will ye reply: "You do but illustrate
> The Iron laws that chain the will of God"?
> Say ye, o'er that yet quivering mass of flesh:
> "God is avenged: the wage of sin is death"?
> What crime, what sin, had those young hearts conceived
> That lie, bleeding and torn, on mother's breast?
> Did fallen Lisbon deeper drink of vice
> Than London, Paris, or sunlit Madrid?[2]

---

2. From *Toleration and Other Essays* by Voltaire. Translated, with an Introduction, by Joseph McCabe (New York: G. P. Putnam's Sons, 1912).

A few years later, in chapter 5 of his novel, *Candide,* Voltaire reiterates this position, which became his lifelong stance. In the novel, the protagonist, Candide, is caught in the outskirts of the Lisbon earthquake, and listens in stunned disbelief to his interlocutor, Pangloss, who gives all sorts of abstruse explanations and rationalizations about how this could fit in with a rational order and divine providence.

But it is important to realize that Voltaire's reaction is based on a particular and rather idiosyncratic notion of divine perfection. As David Hart points out:

> Voltaire's poem is not directly concerned with the God of Christian doctrine. Rather, it concerns a God who directly governs a cosmos that is exactly as he intended it (or as he had to intend it), balancing out all its many eventualities and particularities in a sort of infinite equation that leaves no remainder—no irredeemable evil, no irrecuperable absurdity—behind.[3]

Cornelius Hunter, analyzing the disappointment about God common to Voltaire and other *philosophes,* argues that the conviction that God would never permit evils, imperfections, superfluous "vestigial" organs, or monstrosities in the world led not only to deism, but to materialism. In other words, materialism often amounts to "theological naturalism"—motivated by a sanitized and polished concept of a God who would never allow messy, violent, or ugly realities in His creation. The obvious conclusion: only mindless and uncaring material mechanisms could lead to such results![4] Thus God's "honor" would be saved, at the expense of removing him to infinite remoteness—at the most, just starting up the series, and then "letting nature take its course."

In any case, the "problem of evil" remains in contemporary thought as the major disincentive to acceptance of theism. David Ramsay Steele, disagreeing with other atheists about the impossibility of *proving* the non-existence of God, argues that an "all-loving, all-powerful God" who allows "earthquakes and epidemic diseases," even if "engineered by fallen angels" with "free will," is as obviously self-contradictory and non-existent as the giant wasp in H. G. Wells' story, *The Food of the Gods.*[5]

3. David Bentley Hart, *The Doors of the Sea,* 22.

4. Cornelius G. Hunter, *Science's Blind Spot: The Unseen Religion of Scientific Naturalism* (Grand Rapids, Mich.: Brazos Press, 2007).

5. David Ramsay Steele, *Atheism Explained* (Chicago: Open Court, 2008), 168–70.

Whether one's rebellion against evil leads to deism, as with Voltaire, or drives to materialism, as with Baron Paul d'Holbach (1723–89), or to atheism, as with Denis Diderot (1713–84) and many other contemporaries of Voltaire, a flood of unflattering anthropomorphic depictions of the Deity begins to arrive on the scene:

- God the masochist, delighting in pain inflicted for the good it is doing for souls—to "purify" sinful humans.
- God the avenger, punishing sins to the last iota.
- A deity absorbed in absolute bliss, surrounded by cherubim, seraphim, and other courtiers. Reminiscent of Nero fiddling while Rome burns.
- A *deus ex machina,* manipulating the universe toward certain selected goals, and indifferent to the costs from injustices and personal suffering.
- God the super-administrator, only concerned with the major areas, leaving all details to subordinates in an angelic or human hierarchy.
- An arch-perpetrator of child neglect—definitely *not* the God fantasized by superstitious believers (the "little mother" type of God, assiduous at details, rushing to help when His good and faithful children are in need).

These, of course, are extreme anthropomorphic depictions. But can the believer, who rejects such extremes, assert that there is any necessity, or even congruity, in God's allowing, and even seeming to condone, evil in the world? If we in the twenty-first century wanted to flesh out in greater detail, and update, the evils mentioned in general terms by Hume and others, the evils would include (1) *natural evils,* from the earthquake at Lisbon in the eighteenth century to the December 2004 tsunami in Indonesia, the August 2004 hurricane on the Gulf Coast of the United States, the 1976 Tangshan and 2008 Sichuan earthquakes in China, responsible for over three hundred thousand deaths and the 2010 earthquake that devastated Haiti; (2) *humanly instigated* atrocities and massacres, such as the "final solutions" and "ethnic cleansings" and mindless "jihads" witnessed during the last hundred years; and (3) incapacitating and apparently meaningless congenital *physical and mental inflictions,* especially on humans who have done nothing to bring these sufferings on themselves—for example, the pain and tremors and lack of control connected with multiple sclerosis, or the disorientation and social alienation experienced by a schizophrenic.

In what follows, for purposes of clarity, rather than trying to address the problem of "evil" as an umbrella term, I will consider each of these three different categories of evils separately.

NATURAL EVILS

Planetary Geological and Meteorological Events

Under the category of "natural evils"—or their infelicitous synonym, "acts of God"—most people would list events like earthquakes, tsunamis, avalanches, volcanic eruptions, tornadoes, hurricanes, lightning strikes, wildfires, and lethal changes of weather in terms of hot and cold extremes. Scientists who have studied the evolution of the earth portray these natural developments as minor episodes in the context of the innumerable cataclysmic events taking place in the universe after the big bang. As mentioned in the previous section, the common reaction of cosmologists and astronomers is admiration for the incredible "fine-tuning" of the cosmos. The denizens of planet earth might wish that the cataclysms would subside in their minuscule vicinity—but can anyone imagine a scenario that would completely lack meteorite crashes, lightning, hurricanes, tornadoes, earthquakes, etc.? Indubitably, this scenario would require constant miracles, either quashing natural forces—for example, inhibiting the movements of tectonic plates to prevent earthquakes or reducing the speed of the earth's rotation to minimize the meteorological conditions that bring on hurricanes—with all the attendant side effects resulting from such interdictions (for example, without wildfires, phosphorous and potassium would remain within trees unavailable for plant growth, and without movable tectonic plates, no life on earth would be possible)[6] or, alternatively, we might visualize constant angelic-like interventions, removing individuals from danger, or removing dangers from individuals and communities in timely fashion—for example, stopping mudslides over houses in California that had been built on mountainsides to get a better view, or stopping flooding over buildings below sea level near the coast of New Orleans.

6. See Peter Ward and Donald Brownlee, *Rare Earth: Why Complex Life Is Uncommon in the Universe* (New York: Springer-Verlag, 2000), 194, 220.

Such constant interventions would certainly not be countenanced by philosophers denying the possibility, or even the feasibility, of divine interventions, compromising the efficacy of the laws of nature. And not only philosophers, but most of mankind, would maintain that it is the part of rational beings to become aware of the vicissitudes of nature and take appropriate protective measures to avoid disastrous consequences.

The light amid the shadows of natural disasters is obvious: without the possibility of "acts of God," there would be minimal or no motivation for understanding the secrets of nature, controlling the environment, and improving the living conditions of society, generation by generation. Because of our awareness of such untoward possibilities, architects and engineers learn to construct buildings and infrastructures to withstand the elements and stresses, chemists have investigated the properties and interactions of fundamental elements, geologists and seismologists are achieving a greater understanding of the movements of tectonic plates giving rise to earthquakes, meteorologists develop early-warning systems for hurricanes and tsunamis, and agronomists investigate the properties of climate and soil that are necessary for avoiding the destruction of crops.

In fact, our present understanding of the evolution of the cosmos, the planet, and life should make it easier for us, living in the twenty-first century, to understand the unavoidability of natural evils, than for someone living in previous eras, believing in the literal biblical version of creation, with no knowledge of meteorites passing in the vicinity of the earth, the causes of hurricanes and tsunamis, etc. A world without "natural evils," in which humans were gently prevented from moving into areas with unhealthy or dangerous climatic patterns, and in which no sudden movements of the earth causing earthquakes took place, all sudden changes in weather systems were controlled, and all plants and animals dangerous to life and limb were miraculously sequestered, would be a lotus land, too good to be true, too controlled to be real. It is conceivable that some would prefer this genre of idyllic existence, somewhat reminiscent of the description of paradise in Genesis. With a little imagination, we can conjecture that possibly this sort of continual divine or angelic intervention actually took place in the world of "Adam." But needless to say, something happened. If there ever was such a virtual protective terrestrial womb, it was removed. Humans now must encounter nature, learn the secrets of the elements, gradually control what can be controlled, and learn to avoid what can't be controlled.

Biological Disorder and Violence

In the mind of others, "natural evils" would include principally what Tennyson referred to as "nature, red in tooth and claw"[7]—the often bloody struggle for life that we commonly associate with Darwinian "survival of the fittest."

Cornelius Hunter focuses on Darwin's theory of evolution as a concerted attempt to solve the problem of biological evil. Like Voltaire in the eighteenth-century Enlightenment, and many in the Victorian age, Darwin seemed to tentatively harbor a concept of a God above all evil, creating harmonies in the universe after a Newtonian model, and certainly above and beyond the cruelty, waste, maladaptations, apparently useless organs, etc. that Darwin as a naturalist was constantly encountering in his research and expeditions. Rather than attribute the apparent chaos and *mis*management of the natural world to a good and wise God, Darwin came to see the innumerable random developments of "natural selection" as the most cogent explanation for such natural evils:

> Creation [in the Victorian age] was not viewed as groaning under the weight of sin but rather was expected to be harmonious and perfect. So idealistic were the Victorians' expectations that even unsprouted seeds were a problem. It seemed that God and nature were at strife. . . . Nature seemed to lack precision and economy in design and was not befitting of the Creator. There were birds that laid a bounty of eggs only to have many rot, and there was the "strange and odious instinct" of the young cuckoo bird that ejected its siblings from the nest. Bees destroyed themselves with their sting and produced drones in vast numbers for one single act, only then to be slaughtered by their sisters. There must have been some other explanation for all this confusion; Darwin could hardly imagine that his good God was behind "the clumsy, wasteful, blundering, low, and horribly cruel works of nature."[8]

If we were to carry the Victorian idea of a "good God," working harmoniously and efficiently and gently in nature, to its logical extremes,

---

7. Alfred Lord Tennyson, *In Memoriam* LVI, 1087.
8. Cornelius Hunter, *Darwin's God* (Grand Rapids, Mich.: Brazos Press, 2001), 140.

the result would be a *reductio ad absurdum*. Just to reduce the blood-letting in nature, the creation of carnivorous species would have to be eliminated, the food chain as we know it would disappear, and human nature would need to be re-engineered; and the disposal of dead bodies would turn out to be a monumental task, perhaps the main occupation of most human beings. As Geoffrey Simmons observes, regarding the massive "recycling mechanisms" taking place at all times on the earth:

> Some recyclers perish or are eaten so that the next shift can do their work—the price of business. Others linger for generations. They come in waves or shifts in a definite order with specific job descriptions, and they know how to utilize their tools, which include enzymes, heat, water, and oxygen. Flesh tends to belong to one group, bodily fluids to another, and hair or bones to still another. There are the first responders, the intermediate crews, and the final-touchers. They have their unique agenda, driven by survival, and without their combined and coordinated efforts, we would be climbing over mountains of dead animals from eons ago, sloshing through new excrement, and stepping on fossilized excrement of all kinds, swimming among billions of dead fish, crabs, and algae, drinking opaque slurries of various excrement and microorganisms, breathing air loaded with dried cells and flecks of animal waste, driving over stacked-up roadkill that had been smashed a thousand times over, and farming amidst monstrous mounds of dead crops. Life would not be pleasant.[9]

It is difficult to imagine a God using a "top-down" approach to work out all such "recycling" details, in order to avoid an even messier situation. It seemed reasonable—even for many theists—to conclude to a "laissez-faire" interpretation, explaining the mysterious and sometimes unaesthetic and often inconvenient vicissitudes of nature in terms of the lower-level competition for food and defense and progeny that was required for "survival of the fittest." But, needless to say, the administrator-God that remained after these theistic revisions, although perhaps deserving of respect and admiration for starting up the engines of creation, retained at most a rather solipsistic sort of "goodness"—hard to reconcile with the traditional Christian concept of a loving and provident God whose goodness was diffused and reflected in nature.

9. *Billions of Missing Links* (Eugene, Oreg.: Harvest House, 2007), 147–48.

It is worth noting that other evolutionists, less engrossed in evils and apparent mistakes in nature, came up with a different "reading" of evolution. Alfred Russel Wallace, Darwin's contemporary and co-discoverer of evolution, interpreted natural selection in a teleological fashion, and his later interest in spiritualism seemed to be motivated by this perception of purposefulness in evolution. The Jesuit paleontologist Teilhard de Chardin, following the lead of the French philosopher Henri Bergson, not only interpreted evolution in a teleological sense, and theorized about the physical bases for evolution, but even saw evolutionary processes as a proof of the existence of a personal God.[10] In his masterwork, *The Phenomenon of Man,*[11] defending evolution as the theory to which all other physical theories have to remain subordinate, he portrays a purposeful upward development of the species to higher complexity and concomitant higher "centricity," including the ultimate "centricity" of consciousness and union with "Omega God." Not completely ignoring evil, he adds an appendix to his book, "Some Remarks on the Place and Part of Evil in a World in Evolution." In a few pages he ascribes the existence of evils to the trial-and-error groping inherent in evolutionary growth, describes the panoply of evolutionary development as a "Way of the Cross," and poses the rhetorical question as to whether, from a Christian viewpoint, the impression we get of almost an "excess" of evil might not be due to some primordial event like original sin.[12] But the main characteristic of Teilhard's analyses, throughout his books and articles on evolution, is an admiration for the grandeur of upward biological progress to human consciousness and even beyond, to the futuristic development of a collective "noosphere" covering the earth.

One does not have to accept Teilhard's controversial theory to see further evidence in his "reading" of evolution that—just as beauty is to some extent in the "eye of the beholder"—so also the discernment of good and evil in the phenomena of nature is subject to interpretation. I once published an article entitled "The Problem of Good."[13] In this article, I argued that the concentration by philosophers on the

10. Pierre Teilhard de Chardin, *Human Energy,* trans. J. M. Cohen (New York: Harcourt Brace Jovanovich, 1962), 43, 46, 151.

11. *The Phenomenon of Man,* Introduction by Sir Julian Huxley, trans. Bernard Wall (New York: Harper Torchbooks, 1961).

12. Ibid., 311.

13. H. Kainz, "Immateriality, Teleology, and the Problem of Good," *Contemporary Philosophy* 11, no. 6, fall 1986.

"problem of evil" is caused by our characteristic emphasis on the material at the expense of the spiritual, and on mechanical interactions, searching for causal mechanisms rather than looking to teleology and the "big picture." One does not have to be a hopelessly optimistic person to see that there is all manner of goodness in the world. Even the inveterate materialist should be able at times to view the universe, not just as a collection of exploding supernovas, colliding galaxies, etc., but as a panoply of beauty and harmony; and at times admire the millions of colorful varieties of flora, the tender care of their young by the wildest and most ferocious animals, and especially the beauty and goodness of humans, physically and psychologically and intellectually.

Metaphysically and even semantically, one cannot understand evil except in the context of good. Only if we are able to perceive, like Teilhard, the immense goodness in the upward ascent of evolution, can we best put the bloody and seemingly chaotic aspects of nature into proper perspective.

MORAL EVILS

If those who speak about the incompatibility of the existence of God with evil in the world are referring to *moral* evil—that is, human acts that are malicious and cause evil—the apologist in God's corner has a much easier time of it. For presumably no one would seriously wish that God had created humans as automatons without freedom. If someone were to maintain that God could have created free rational beings, but without the possibility of committing evil, they would be involved in a *contradictio in adjecto,* advocating a freedom without freedom. They would be visualizing, *per impossibile,* incarnate rational creatures without the possibility of *hurting* others—that is, every act that might cause malicious hurt or pain for another would have to be inhibited; possibly even the *thought* of doing such acts would be made impossible. Humans under such interdictions would have to be like robots, doing only what they are programmed to do, and worthy neither of praise nor blame for any of their decisions or actions.

The only possible scenario conceivable in which individuals would be free, but prevented from doing evil, would be the sort of autobiographical experience that Socrates reports in Plato's dialogue, the *Apology*. Socrates claimed to have had, from childhood, a divine voice that would oppose him even "in quite trivial things" if he were to take the wrong course, entering into activities or commitments that were not good; this voice did not actually prevent him from making wrong choices, but "dissuaded" him, and Socrates claimed that he was always voluntarily obedient to the voice.[14] This extraordinary, anomalous, ostensibly supernatural sort of experience may be akin to the sort of experience that is reported in Genesis, when Adam and Eve were warned not to eat of the "tree of knowledge of good and evil" but were allowed to freely choose to ignore this warning.[15] The counterpart of this voice, available to the rest of us mortals, is the "voice of conscience." The implantation of conscience in rational and free creatures by God might stand as a suitable response to those who ask, "Why doesn't God do something to prevent *moral* evils"?

We are living in an era when technological progress has produced, as a "side effect," the development of nuclear, biological, and chemical weaponry, thus opening up the possibility of stupendous crimes on a scale scarcely imaginable in previous centuries: wholesale massacres, genocides, obliteration of nations. Unfortunately, in the contemporary world, some of these crimes are being committed in the name of religion. But it is not only religious people who have developed the advanced capability of ignoring the voice of conscience. As Berlinsky observes, recounting some of the "highlights" of the twentieth century:

> It was not religion or religious people who "imposed on the suffering human race poison gas, barbed wire, high explosives, experiments in eugenics, the formula for Zyklon B, heavy artillery, pseudo-scientific justifications for mass murder, cluster bombs, attack submarines, napalm, intercontinental ballistic missiles, military space platforms, and nuclear weapons.[16]

Is free will so sacrosanct that God would not intervene by force, restraining evil individuals from acts that would remove the possibility of freedom for millions or billions of people? Possibly, like leaders and administrators who adhere to the "principle of subsidiarity," God would prioritize other methods, consonant with freedom, and dependent on other free individuals, for defending against such "worst-case scenarios." God, like us, may not want to give up on the idea of free will.

14. Plato, *Apology* 31c–32a; 40a–40c.
15. Gn 2:17.
16. David Berlinski, *Devil's Delusion,* 21.

NATURAL CONGENITAL SUFFERING

It is the increased consciousness of the overwhelming presence of pain and suffering in the world that ordinarily leads to the intensified complaint: "How could a good God allow such things?" This question becomes particularly acute with regard to people who seem to have been "born" into suffering.

Sufferings caused by insects, bacteria, plants, and animals, and by "acts of God," have already been considered above under the rubric of "natural evils." Sufferings caused by other people have also been considered above in the discussion of "moral evils." "Moral evils" also give rise to physical suffering in oneself or others—for example, AIDS transmitted to one's children, or mental/neurological diseases or disabilities caused by a parent's drug use or alcoholism; and also the plethora of sufferings caused by one's own moral delinquencies—for example, cirrhosis of the liver caused by alcoholism, lung cancer from smoking, STDs from promiscuity, as well as the side effects of drug use and the numerous maladies caused by overindulgence in food and drink.

The third and distinct problem area of "natural congenital suffering" that I am now referring to is limited to diseases caused not by external human or environmental agents, but by hereditary factors, genetic "markers," or by still unknown causes that seem to be lurking in the human organism. With regard to such cases, the problem about God's providence boils down to the questions: "Why wouldn't God manipulate the genetic code so that such conditions would never appear?" and "What particular good would have to be sacrificed if God were to obliterate this type of evil?"

Those who see such conditions as evils that a good God should have prevented may think that God could "tweak" the human genetic makeup to make these types of suffering disappear, without causing genetic side effects with unexpected disastrous results. But this is doubtful. For example, the same gene that caused resistance to malaria for blacks in West Africa also caused susceptibility to sickle-cell anemia for their descendants in the United States. Can we presuppose that some sort of "tweaking" of the genetic code could have maintained the benefits for the former and removed the disadvantages for the latter? Such a presupposition would require biological knowledge unavailable now or in the near future.

It probably will not soothe the doubts of skeptics to remind them that, without diseases and the sufferings they bring, the world's knowledge of the makeup and dynamics of the human body would be minimal. The search for cures of diseases has led to the search for their causes. It is hardly conceivable that the discovery of DNA and the massive commitment of world resources to the recently completed worldwide Genome Project has not been conditioned in great part by the quest to discover the causes of hereditary diseases. Of course, many would be willing to forgo such scientific advances, if human genetics could be rewired to prevent natural congenital suffering without any attendant evil side effects. But, as indicated above, even a super-geneticist might find that to be unachievable.

A World Without Pain and Suffering?: Some Reflections

Numerous examples exist of individuals who have come to terms with suffering, made a pact with it, and even place it in a positive light. For athletes, the truism/motto is "no pain, no gain." Runners, swimmers, weightlifters, wrestlers, and bikers subject themselves to gigantic ordeals of pain and deprivations in order to attain a desired degree of strength and endurance. Not to be outdone by athletes, intellectuals in all eras have voluntarily endured rigid regimes of study and research, leading to the exasperated maxim, "Knowledge maketh a bloody entrance." Ascetics in all major religions have voluntarily chosen deprivations and self-inflicted sufferings with the goal of perfecting themselves spiritually. And all sorts of ordinary people have attained self-control and solid virtues through persistent, patient dealings with their individualized sufferings.

Would a life completely without pain be a boon? Definitely not. The rare disease, CIPA (congenital insensitivity to pain with anhidrosis), offers such a life. A child is born who has only the sensations of pressure and touch, and never perspires, but feels no pain, not even internal warning signals like the urgency of a full bladder. The initial discovery of this disease by parents or caregivers is usually through traumatic experiences—for example, a baby bites off part of its tongue when it is teething. Children growing up with CIPA will often bite off their own finger, or blind themselves by putting their finger in their eye, or put their hand in a fire, resulting in third-degree burns, or break their toes by bumping into things, or cut themselves and look puzzled at the blood spurting out, or jump from a high place, breaking arms or legs. This is a dangerous disease. The average lifespan is twenty-five years. Heart attacks are not felt, nor a ruptured appendix.

Pain thus is necessary for the avoidance of injuries to the organism. But if the philosopher Unamuno is correct, it also has an existential function. He raises the question of how we gain intensely concrete (not just anatomical) knowledge of the parts of our own body, and finds suffering to be an indispensable element for this understanding:

> Although in deference to authority we may believe, we do not in fact know, that we possess heart, stomach, or lungs so long as they do not cause us discomfort, suffering, or anguish. Physical suffering, or even discomfort, is what reveals to us our own internal core.[17]

And Unamuno proposes a thought experiment designed to lead us to an understanding of the existential importance of suffering:

> Which would you find most appalling—to feel such a pain as would deprive you of your senses on being pierced through with a white-hot iron, or to see yourself thus pierced through without feeling any pain? Have you never felt the horrible terror of feeling yourself incapable of suffering and of tears? Suffering tells us that we exist.[18]

This is not an apologetic for masochism. The strange fascination that a masochist has for pain might be explained as an attempt to achieve a more intense experience of his own existence. Such fixations help to illustrate Unamuno's point. But his argument is geared to the ordinary person dealing with the unavoidable "slings and arrows" of life.

THEODICY AND THE PROBLEM OF EVIL

In a sense, Christianity gave rise to "theodicy" as a *philosophical* discipline. Christianity from its inception has placed such persistent emphasis on the goodness of God and His love for all humanity that it is no wonder that, at certain junctures when the evils in the world seem to "give the lie" to any such presumed goodness, Christian

---

17. Miguel de Unamuno, *Tragic Sense of Life* (New York: Dover Publications, 1954), 212.
18. Ibid., 207.

philosophers might take it upon themselves to "justify the ways of God to men." One such philosopher was Leibniz, who coined the term "theodicy" and who elicited the famous outrage of Voltaire, discussed at the outset of this chapter. When Leibniz argued for the "best-possible-world" theory that Voltaire found so objectionable, he used mathematical and geometrical analogies concerning the necessity of maximum and minimum[19] and the relation between whole and part,[20] and he concluded with a summary of how God, presuming He had an omniscient grasp of all "possibles," could have indeed made calculations producing the best world possible:

> The infinity of possibles, however great it may be, is no greater than that of the wisdom of God, who knows all possibles. . . . The wisdom of God, not content with embracing all the possibles, penetrates them, compares them, weighs them one against the other, to estimate their degrees of perfection or imperfection, the strong and the weak, the good and the evil. It goes even beyond the finite combinations, it makes of them an infinity of infinites, that is to say, an infinity of possible sequences of the universe, each of which contains an infinity of creatures. By this means the divine Wisdom distributes all the possibles it had already contemplated separately, into so many universal systems which it further compares the one with the other. The result of all these comparisons and deliberations is the choice of the best from among all these possible systems, which wisdom makes in order to satisfy goodness completely.[21]

An updated version of Leibniz' theory that God created the best world (that is, with the least amount of evil, and the greatest amount of good) might use, instead of the mathematical analogies that Leibniz himself used, the analogy of current efforts at computer-aided medical decision making (for example, by developing decision-trees calculated to result in the best possible outcome for the patient). We might conjecture that God, knowing all the contingent developments in nature and all the choices of humans, would be able to fashion the best of all possible worlds even from recalcitrant materials, bringing about the best possible outcome for each individual (in this life and/or an afterlife), and even when the slightest mistake could lead to the extinction of mankind through a disaster, nuclear or other-

19. G. W. Leibniz, *Theodicy: Essays on the Goodness of God, the Freedom of Man, and the Origin of Evil*, trans. E. M. Huggard (New Haven: Yale University Press, 1952), 128.

20. Ibid., 260.

21. Ibid., 267–68.

wise. This portrayal would be in tandem with the occasional comments of cosmologists that "God would have to be a mathematician."

Other philosophers have followed the lead of Leibniz, but without the emphasis on mathematics. The German philosopher G. W. F. Hegel (1770–1831), in his *Philosophy of History*, berates theologians who continually make inspirational references to the "providence of God" without ever trying to work out a "*theodicaea*" demonstrating with rational argument just how this providence is still maintained amid all the evils rampant in the world.[22] Hegel then embarked on the task of attempting precisely this, starting with ancient oriental empires, analyzing the emergence of the consciousness of freedom in ancient and medieval civilizations, and arriving ultimately at a consideration of the high point of this consciousness in the then-contemporary European civilization. In his *Phenomenology of Spirit*, Hegel takes a somewhat different but complementary approach to theodicy: reacting against the common notion of a transcendent deity outside the world, he portrays God as a World Spirit, operating in and through men, and suffering in and through them. The history of the world is thus conceptualized as a macrocosmic expansion of the passion of the Christ, a Golgotha in which humans complete the sufferings necessary for the World Spirit to attain the Absolute.[23] This latter approach, emphasizing the immanence of God in world developments, avoids questions about an aloof God outside the world permitting evil in the world.

Similarly, and more recently, "process philosophers" locate the Deity squarely within the world, suffering with the world, and striving persuasively to enlist the cooperation and collaboration of all entities to bring about the best outcomes, as far as possible. In Charles Hartshorne's formulation, God as the necessary being, and creatures as contingent, are necessarily related to each other, almost as form and content, intertwined in the process of divine emergence and the suffering this entails.[24] Teilhard de Chardin presents a somewhat similar picture, updated to incorporate the theory of evolution, in which God as the final "Omega" end point of evolution is immanent in the

22. See G. W. F. Hegel, *The Philosophy of History*, Sibree trans. (New York: Dover, 1956), 15.

23. See G. W. F. Hegel, *Phenomenology of Mind*, Baillie trans. (New York: Harper Torchbooks, 1967), 808.

24. See Charles Hartshorne, *Omnipotence and Other Theological Mistakes* (Albany: State University of New York, 1984), 82–83.

material world, directing the processes through all the periods of "growth," which necessarily involve suffering.[25]

THEOLOGICAL CONSIDERATIONS

In the Judeo-Christian tradition, the origin of evil in the world is traced back to Satan, a fallen angel so intelligent and so powerful that he once considered himself equal to God. One might wonder why Satan, after being expelled from heaven with his angelic cohorts, would be permitted by God to be the archetypal master of chaos and destruction, instead of being confined to some outer darkness and prohibited from evildoing, or even annihilated. But the rationale seems to be that, just as God allows humans to exercise their freedom maliciously, so also the devils, although being subjected to temporary restraints,[26] are allowed to continue in conflict with angels and humans, in a process in which humans must align themselves with one side or the other. Satan has the undeniable ability and freedom to work havoc in this struggle. When Satan asked Yahweh for permission to afflict Job and his family physically, the permission was granted, with a proviso about sparing Job's life.[27] When Satan took Jesus up to a high mountain, and offered him unlimited wealth and power, Jesus did not deny that the devil possessed the ability to confer such things, but simply replied that he wanted none of it.[28] Presumably Satan, unlike humans, has privileged information about who has been saved and who hasn't, and about exactly what sorts of things were effective in bringing about their salvation or the lack of it. And the ability of the "father of lies"[29] to appear to the unwary as an "angel of light"[30] is perhaps his greatest asset in his quest for enlisting humans to collaborate in the proliferation of chaos and destruction.

In the Christian tradition, of course, the initial success of Satan is interconnected with the doctrine of original sin. As an innate disruption of the optimal harmony of inclinations and desires in the psyche, original sin offers a partial explanation for the host of moral

25. *The Phenomenon of Man*, 309–11.
26. See, for example, Rev 20:2, 7.
27. Jb 1:12, 2:6.
28. Mt 4:8–9.
29. Jn 8:44.
30. 2 Cor 11:14.

evils that are ascribed to uncontrolled and irrational passions. Even non-Christians may gather some empirical evidence of original sin from their observations of the dark side of human nature—*homo homini lupus.*

An antidote to despair about the prevalence of evil in the world is the promise of eternal life after death. This doctrine is dimly adumbrated in the Old Testament[31] but clearly and emphatically revealed throughout the New Testament. The "good news" conveyed by the Gospel is primarily about Christ's victory over death and the assurance of resurrection in eternal life. Thus, for Christians, the problem of suffering is diminished or nullified because of this hope, the "eyes on the prize." Says Paul, "I consider that the sufferings of this present time are as nothing compared with the glory to be revealed for us."[32] And Peter: "Rejoice to the extent that you share in the sufferings of Christ, so that when his glory is revealed you may also rejoice exultantly."[33] In fact, among saints and ascetics, the supposition is that some joys of the afterlife will be directly related to the sufferings of this life, and the types and sources of suffering will be transformed into the marks and crowns of glory, as the wounds of Christ appeared as glorified insignia after his resurrection.[34]

It is in terms of such presuppositions that Aquinas offers arguments about divine providence that would not be made by philosophers under the rubric of mere "theodicy" but that make sense from a Christian viewpoint: "If all evil were prevented, much good would be absent from the universe. . . . There would be no patience of martyrs if there were no tyrannical persecution";[35] and "There would be no patience of the righteous, if there were no ill-will of the persecutors."[36]

The promise of eternal life in the Christian dispensation, of course, brings with it the possibility of hell as the alternative. This gives rise to the usual questions about the justice of God: How could a good God condemn anyone to eternal punishment? Shouldn't His often-acclaimed infinite mercy be able to redeem even those who have murdered, plundered, lied their way through life, mocked God and religion? But the question should be formulated differently. The

---

31. See, for example, 1 Sm 2:6, Jb 19:25, Ps 16:10, Dn 12:2–3.
32. Rom 8:18.
33. 1 Pt 4:13.
34. Lk 24:39–40, Jn 20:27.
35. *S. T.* I, q. 22, a. 2, ad 10.
36. *Summa contra gentiles* III, 71.

right question, in view of free will, should be whether someone who has resisted God and perpetrated evil throughout his life could voluntarily enter into a kingdom of universal love, which heaven is supposed by Christians to be. Certainly all the free-will acts of a person's life produce habitual attitudes. Could such attitudes and the commitments they engender be simply overcome at the time of death?

Implications of the Incarnation

If we accept the inevitability of the three types of evils discussed above, the Christian message of a God becoming human in order to experience and share in our world in spite of these evils would seem to be the most acceptable answer, or at least the least objectionable answer, to the question of how the goodness of God is compatible with the prevalence of evil. For those who accept Jesus Christ as the incarnate God-man, the notion of an aloof, indifferent, unconcerned deity caught up in solitary bliss while creatures suffer and die is dissipated. Tertullian's comment, often incorrectly paraphrased as "I believe because it is absurd," is most relevant to this belief:

> The Son of God was born—something not to be ashamed of, since it is so shameful. And the Son of God died—something completely believable, since it was so unfitting. And, having been buried, he arose—something to be certain of, since it was so impossible.[37]

Christianity, in which the almighty and eternal God descends to earth to fully partake in human life, and experience the dregs of suffering and death, is clearly more "unbelievable" than any other religion. As Tertullian observes, it is patently absurd that God—at least, God as He is usually pictured or conceptualized—would do such a thing. But someone who believes all these "unbelievable" things cannot help but have his whole perspective, regarding a sometimes hostile world and the evils of life, overturned. Evil, thus revised, is not as bad as the devil.

---

37. Tertullian, *De carne Christi* 5:4: "*Natus est Dei Filius; non pudet, quia pudendum est: et mortuus est Dei Filius; prorsus credible est, quia ineptum est: et sepultus resurrexit; certum est, quia impossibile.*" (Some references to this passage have "*Crucifixus est Dei Filius . . .*," but the *Patrologia Latina* reads "*Natus est Dei Filius . . .*"

3

The Characteristics of God

You have disposed all things by measure and number and weight.
For with you great strength abides always; who can resist the might
of your arm? . . . But you have mercy on all, because you can do
all things; and you overlook the sins of men that they may repent.
—Wisdom 11:20–22

His mercy is from age to age to those who fear him. He has shown
might with his arm, dispersed the arrogant of mind and heart. He
has thrown down the rulers from their thrones but lifted up the
lowly. The hungry he has filled with good things, the rich he has
sent away empty. He has helped Israel his servant, remembering
his mercy, according to his promise to our fathers, to Abraham
and to his descendants forever.
—Luke 1:50–55

St. PAUL, CONFRONTING THE GREEKS AT THE AREOPAGUS, PRESUMED
that the multiple shrines dedicated to various deities demonstrated
that the Greeks were committed to worshipping God; but the very
multiplicity of shrines showed they were uncertain about any characteristics beyond mere existence. The altar "to an unknown God" provided Paul with the opportunity to try to clarify what this God that
they were unknowingly worshipping was really like. Present at Paul's
preaching was an Athenian named Dionysius, who became a follower
of Paul and one of the first bishops. In the fourth or fifth century, a
Neoplatonist philosopher, Pseudo-Dionysius, took up what he considered to be the mantle of the biblical Dionysius, and tried to go
even further than Paul in giving a mystical interpretation of the divine characteristics, in a book entitled *The Divine Names*. Thomas
Aquinas, along with many other medieval scholastics, thinking that
The Divine Names was the work of the sainted contemporary of Paul,
ascribed maximum authority to it, but with some reservations. While

64

the approach of Pseudo-Dionysius was through a "negative theology," which claimed that we can ascribe "names" to God only through a process of negation (describing what God is *not*), Aquinas took a more moderate position, emphasizing that various references to God as good, infinite, simple, immutable, eternal, etc. are justified as analogies, containing positive meaning, although with all the limitations attendant on analogical discourse.[1] Following Aquinas, we may note that all attempts to specify positive characteristics of God must proceed through analogies.

CLARIFICATION OF GOD'S CHARACTERISTICS IN THE HISTORY OF PHILOSOPHY

The attempt to offer suitable analogical characterizations of God began in Western philosophy with the Pre-Socratics. For example, the Greek philosopher, Xenophanes (ca. 570–470 B.C.) declares that:

> God is one, supreme among gods and men, not at all like mortals in body or in mind. . . . Without effort he sets everything in motion by the thought of his mind. He always abides in the selfsame place, not moving at all; it is not appropriate to his nature to be in different places at different times.[2]

And Empedocles (ca. 490–430 B.C.) describes God as "purely mind, holy and ineffable, flashing through the whole world with swift thoughts."[3]

Plato (428–348 B.C.) argued for the existence of God from the order in nature and in natural law,[4] and went on to hypothesize that God governs the passage of the universe through all time,[5] is responsible for all the good in the world,[6] and speaks through poets and prophets.[7]

Aristotle (384–322 B.C.), arguing for the existence of God as the origin of all movement in the world,[8] speculated that God, remaining immobile "self-thinking thought,"[9] causes all the movements through

1. Cf. *S.T.* I, q. 13, a. 5.
2. See Philip Wheelwright, ed., *The Presocratics* (New York: Odyssey Press, 1966), 32, frag. 1–4.
3. Ibid., 140, frag. 80.
4. *Laws,* 885–86.
5. *Laws* IV, 715.
6. *Republic* II, 379.
7. *Ion,* 534.
8. See *Physics* VIII, 6, 259a, 3 ff.
9. Aristotle, *Metaphysics* XII, 1072b, 23–26.

the various concentric "spheres" of the cosmos by being loved.[10] In other words, as the supremely attractive being, he activates the will and appetites of subordinate spiritual substances (considered by Aquinas to be the philosophical equivalent to angels) governing the cosmological spheres, initiating movements that eventually filter down into all levels of the cosmos, including the "sublunary" sphere where our earthly existence is situated.[11] Aristotle also conjectured that there is something like divine providence in the world, analogous to the care that the leaders of an army will exert in planning and ordering what takes place in a purposeful fashion:

> We must consider . . . in which of two ways the nature of the universe contains the good and the highest good, whether as something separate and by itself, or as the order of the parts. Probably in both ways, as an army does; for its good is found both in the order and in the leader, and more in the latter; for he does not depend on the order but it depends on him. And all things are ordered together somehow, but not all alike,—both fishes and fowls and plants; and the world is not such that one thing has nothing to do with another, but they are connected. For all are ordered together to one end.[12]

Later philosophers in the ancient world, still not yet affected by Christian concepts, nevertheless converged with Christian thinkers in ascribing positive qualities to the Deity. For example, the Stoic philosopher Epictetus (60–138 A.D.) held that God is the Father of mankind,[13] the Administrator of the World,[14] who assigns each individual a place in the world, and apportions life-spans for all persons.[15]

IMPLICATIONS OF SOME CONTEMPORARY APPROACHES

The physicist Eugene Wigner, in a 1960 paper, expressed admiration and a bit of befuddlement at the fact that mathematics, far from being relegated to some abstract realm of thought, is broadly incorpo-

---

10. Ibid., 1072b, 3.

11. Ibid., 1073a, 23ff.

12. Aristotle, *Metaphysics* XII, 1075a, 24.

13. *The Golden Sayings of Epictetus*, trans. Hastings Crossley, Harvard Classics Edition (New York: P. F. Collier & Sons, 1937), IX, 120.

14. Ibid., XVI, 122.

15. Ibid., XVIII, 123.

rated in the physical world and in physical interactions.[16] Mario Livio, in *Is God a Mathematician?*, recognizes possible implications about design in Wigner's befuddlement, and searches for explanations based on the evolution of the human brain confronting patterns and regularities in nature, as an alternative to a "mathematical" God.[17] But from the frequent references to mathematical probabilities and improbabilities that have been mentioned in chapter 1 regarding proofs for God's existence, one might reasonably conclude that, if an intelligent Creator was involved, he would certainly have mathematical propensities as an inseparable part of his "personality profile." Physicist Paul Dirac emphasizes this aspect, theorizing that "God is a mathematician of a very high order" who "used very advanced mathematics in constructing the universe."[18] In Catholic and Orthodox versions of the Wisdom books of the Old Testament, it is said that God "disposed all things by measure and number and weight."[19] This may offer some scriptural corroboration for theistically oriented arguments from cosmology, but—without detracting from the mathematical profession or the notion of a "mathematical" personality—most seekers would fondly hope for more universal, less specialized, personality characteristics from the Deity.

Proponents of Intelligent Design and others who discern evidence of purposefulness in the evolution of the species, and imply the existence of a deity on this basis, would perhaps conclude to somewhat different personality characteristics. The God emerging from such a view of biological evolution would best be characterized as a Designer/Artist/Architect, making the best use of all raw materials—human and nonhuman, natural effects and voluntary human choices, including even chaotic and cataclysmic events—to produce what a truly objective observer, transcending space and time, would consider a work of beauty. But the difficulty of glimpsing these qualities, on the part of those of us heavily rooted in space and time, will simply underline the fact that even those who assert the existence of a deity, using all the powers of analogy, may find it difficult to substantiate any humanly attractive personal qualities in God on the basis of reason alone.

16. "The Unreasonable Effectiveness of Mathematics in the Natural Sciences," *Communications in Pure and Applied Mathematics* 13, no. 1 (February 1960).

17. Mario Livio, *Is God a Mathematician?* (New York: Simon & Schuster, 2009).

18. *Scientific American*, May 1963, 53.

19. Ws 11:20.

USING THE OLD TESTAMENT AS AN AID

The literal meaning of the tetragammon, Jahweh (YHVH), as discussed earlier,[20] incorporates the name that God told to Moses when
asked by Moses what His name was—namely, "He who exists." This
name brings out the fact that, not only does God exist—about which
Moses and the Israelites in the desert of Sinai had no doubt—but
that existence is the *essential characteristic* of God. For those who utilize the name Jahweh in this sense, and who are conscious of their
own limited existence between past and future in space and time, the
reference to unbridled existence, lacking any past and future, may
connote a positive presence throughout space and time—the quality
of omnipresence, if further specification were needed.

We tend to see the qualities of justice and mercy as two opposed
extremes, and those who believe in God will often portray Him as
either predominately just or predominately merciful. But the Old
Testament portrayals of Yahweh show a constant dialectical oscillation between justice and mercy. The *justice* of God is the theme when
Adam and Eve are expelled for their sin from the Garden of Eden;[21]
Cain is expelled after murdering his brother Abel, and sentenced to
be a "restless wanderer on the earth";[22] the builders who wanted to
reach up to heaven with the Tower of Babel were dispersed because
of their pride;[23] Pharaoh is punished for his "hardness of heart" in
refusing to release the Israelites from Egypt;[24] Moses is not allowed
to enter the Promised Land because of initial doubts about God's
command to strike a rock to bring out water in the desert of Zin;[25]
David's adultery is followed by the death of his child;[26] David's pre-
sumptuous census taking results in a pestilence;[27] and the idolatry
and promiscuity of King Solomon are punished by taking away his
kingdom.[28]

Counterbalancing these instances of justice, the *mercy* of God is emphasized when He makes "leather garments" for Adam and Eve, af-

20. See p. 42 above.
21. Gn 3:23.
22. Gn 4:11–12.
23. Gn 11:9.
24. Exodus 7:4ff.
25. Nm 20:12, 27:14; Dt 32:51–52.
26. 2 Sm 12:13ff.
27. 2 Sm 24:10ff.
28. 1 Kgs 11:11.

ter their sin;[29] pledges protection for Cain after he murders Abel, and places a "mark" on him so that he would not be killed in retaliation;[30] moderates his planned punishment of the Sodomites, because of the pleas of Abraham;[31] provides manna and quail[32] and water[33] in the desert for the grumbling followers of Moses; postpones and mitigates the loss of Solomon's kingdom out of compassion for the line of David;[34] and through the agency of the major and minor prophets continually modifies His warnings to the Israelites, ravaged by wars and oppression, with demonstrations of compassion and forgiveness.

God in the Old Testament also has an unmistakable propensity for choosing people and situations in a way that is completely at odds with human wisdom. His choice of a patriarch for the chosen people was Abraham, who, childless at one hundred years of age, had no natural hope for any descendants;[35] and it was Abraham's descendants, Israelites reduced to slavery in Egypt,[36] that God chose to make the march into the Promised Land. To lead the Israelites, God chose Moses, a man "slow of speech, and of a slow tongue"[37] because of a speech impediment. For a king to establish Jewish hegemony in Jerusalem, God directed the prophet Samuel to go to the farmer, Jesse, pass over seven of his sons, and anoint the youngest of his sons, David, a simple shepherd who had to be summoned away from herding the sheep;[38] and God chose David, still an adolescent, to defeat the warrior champion of the Philistines, Goliath, with a slingshot.[39]

Using the New Testament

Divine Predilection for the Lowly (Continued)

This divine pattern of choosing humble, ordinary, nondistinguished people and nonprestigious environments continues throughout the

29. Gn 3:21.
30. Gn 4:15.
31. Gn 18:23 ff.
32. Ex 16:4 ff.
33. Ex 17:2 ff.
34. 1 Kgs 11:12.
35. Gn 17:17.
36. Ex 1:13–14.
37. Ex 4:10.
38. 1 Sm 16:11–13.
39. 1 Sm 17:48–51.

New Testament narratives. An obscure Galilean virgin is chosen to be the mother of God's son,[40] whose birth takes place in a stable in Bethlehem;[41] the boy Jesus grows up subject to parents and embedded in an extended family;[42] he learns a trade, and is known to his community as "the carpenter";[43] he conforms to Jewish laws and rituals in all particulars, and submits to baptism from his cousin, John, before beginning his public life;[44] he includes simple fishermen among his apostles[45] and puts one of them in charge of his church;[46] as he travels through Palestine preaching about the Kingdom of God, he performs numerous miraculous healings as evidence of his Messiahship, but assiduously refrains from the ostentatious "signs" that would give him the reputation of a magician, and continually admonishes those whom he has healed against advertising him as a miracle worker;[47] and he is conveyed to his final entry as Messiah into Jerusalem on a borrowed donkey.[48] Finally, as the Christian community began to grow, a rabid Jewish persecutor of Christians, Saul, a poor speaker with an unpleasing appearance,[49] is the unlikely choice as a "vessel of election" to spread the Gospel to the Gentiles, becoming the "Paul" of the New Testament.[50]

Jesus clearly and directly describes his own characteristics at only one place in the Gospels, saying "Learn from me, for I am meek and humble of heart."[51] If one were to encounter Jesus personally, this would no doubt be the main "personality trait" that he might notice. The quality of meekness, however, did not prevent Jesus from criticizing those who personified opposite qualities like conceit and hypocrisy.

Instances of "exalted" appearances of Jesus in the Gospel accounts of his life are rare—a voice coming from heaven in a couple places, and a Transfiguration before a select group of apostles. Most accounts are "low-keyed," portraying a Messiah continually trying to avoid daz-

40. Lk 1:34.
41. Lk 2:7.
42. Lk 2:51.
43. Mt 13:55; Mk 6:3.
44. Mt 3:14–15; 5:17–18.
45. Mt 4:19.
46. Mt 16:18–19; Jn 21:15–17.
47. Mt 8:4; Mk 1:44, 7:36, 8:12, 8:26, 8:30, 9:8; Lk 5:14; 8:56.
48. Jn 12:14.
49. 2 Cor 10:10; 1 Cor 2:4–5.
50. Acts 9:4.
51. Mt 11:19.

zling onlookers with his greatness. If indeed Jesus is God incarnate, offering a visible reflection to us of the divine personality, we may further surmise that God, both in the Old Testament and in the New, does in fact show a preference for choosing individuals with "personality characteristics" similar to his own.

If we consider the major "private revelations" approved by the Catholic Church in the last few centuries, we find a similar pattern. For example, Juan Diego (1474–1548), a simple weaver and laborer living near what is now Mexico City, was chosen by the Virgin Mary to establish the shrine of Guadalupe as a sign of her special patronage for the Americas; Bernadette Soubirous (1844–1879), a weak asthmatic raised in extreme poverty, was chosen by the Virgin to build the shrine at Lourdes, France, noted for a miraculous healing spring; and on May 13, 1917, the Virgin appeared in Fatima, Portugal, to three peasant children—ten-year-old Lucia dos Santos, her cousin Francisco, age nine, and Jacinta Marto, age eight—warning about World War II and the spread of communism, and announcing a series of monthly apparitions that would end on October 13 of the same year with a miracle to authenticate the message.[52]

Credo Quia Absurdum, Reconsidered

At this point, some further extensions of Tertullian's remarks, paraphrased as *credo quia absurdum,* cited in the preceding chapter,[53] may be appropriate. The literal meaning of "I believe because it is absurd" would, of course, be truly absurd. It would mean, "I believe this because I can't believe it." On the other hand, if God followed human logic and common human ideas of power and respectability and *credibility,* the world would perceive a God that was "all too human," and faith would falter.

The positive connotation of *credo quia absurdum* is, then, that divine operations can best be perceived in seemingly "absurd" choices. If a powerful noble in Pharaoh's court had been chosen, instead of Moses, to liberate the Hebrew slaves; if Jonathan, the son of King Saul, who had shown great leadership ability and military prowess, had been chosen instead of David the shepherd; if Jesus were born

---

52. See Stanley Jaki, *God and the Sun at Fatima* (Royal Oak, Mich.: Real View Books, 1999) for a thorough analysis of the events at Fatima in 1917 and depositions of witnesses to the "miracle of the sun."

53. See p. 63 above.

in Herod's palace, and chose Pharisees and Scribes instead of fishermen and tax collectors to help inaugurate the reign of the Messiah;
if a triumphant Jesus had then set up rule in Jerusalem, and a faithful Christian church had continued the traditions he set down with
unbroken apostolic succession, instead of the sometimes bumbling
Roman popes leading the Church in the midst of often chaotic Ital-
ian intrigue; and if worldwide church unity had been summarily established without disintegration and sectarian divisions—this is the
all-too-human way you or I might consider the way to operate divinely,
if we were God, and wanted to establish a Messianic reign on earth.

With regard to the private revelations mentioned above—we don't
know if they are authentic divine messages or not, but we do know
that they would have had minimal credibility if they conformed to human notions of greatness and importance. If, for example, a noted
conquistador instead of Juan Diego had received the miraculous image of the Lady at Guadalupe; or some pious French queen in her
palace, instead of Bernadette in a cave, had seen a vision; or some respectable Portugese children from good families had received the
messages of the Lady about penance and peace, instead of the three
children of Fatima—one cannot even imagine a great impetus to
faith issuing from such events. The lineaments of divine action, going beyond what could conceivably be achieved with human instru-
mentality, would not stand out so clearly in such scenarios.

God as Love

In the first letter of John, toward the end of the Bible, it seems that a
final attempt is being made to offer considerations that will leave no
room for doubt as to the main identifying characteristic of the God
that a Christian believes in:

> Whoever is without love does not know God, for God is love. . . . God is
> love, and whoever remains in love remains in God and God in him.[54]

This epistle, as well as the two epistles of John that follow it, is note-
worthy for emphasizing that the essence of Christianity consists of
love. This is, of course, a message that one finds in the Gospels and
throughout the New Testament. But the apparent identification of

54. 1 Jn 4:8, 4:16.

God with love itself (*ho theos agapê estin*) is unique to John. John is clearly not using synecdoche, describing God in terms of something that John takes to be His chief attribute. He is identifying God with love, and vice versa. And in saying that God is love, he is offering an insight of philosophical import that may help us understand the "how" of God's existence.

One does not have to be a prophet or a poet or even religious to see manifestations of love throughout the universe. Sigmund Freud in *The Ego and the Id* portrays his theory of Eros and Thanatos as "cosmological," insofar as the dualism of love and hate, attraction and repulsion, is present everywhere—in atoms and molecules and cells, as well as in more advanced forms of life.[55] And the Jesuit paleontologist Teilhard de Chardin observes:

> In its most primitive forms, when life was scarcely individualized, love is hard to distinguish from molecular forces; one might think of it as a matter of chemisms or tactisms. Then little by little it becomes distinct, though still *confused* for a very long time with the simple function of reproduction. . . . "Hominized" love is distinct from all other loves. . . . No longer only a unique and periodic attraction for purposes of material fertility; but an unbounded and continuous possibility of contact between minds rather than bodies; the play of countless subtle antennae seeking one another in the light and darkness of the soul.[56]

The ultimate "cosmological" manifestations of love, of course, are in the psychological and social domains, where love is seen in both active and passive forms—as something given to others, or received from others. Interestingly, love in its highest forms is not something substantial and concrete, a thing that could be pointed out or photographed or measured in any way. Though inherent in the physical world, it is largely invisible, like the love that St. John is referring to.

But the love John points to is clearly nonphysical; it is a spiritual unifier that divinizes those who participate in it, or, more precisely, brings the presence of God forcefully into the community. The Gospels spell out the radical difference of this love from all human love by commanding its extension to enemies.[57] And St. Paul points

---

55. See Sigmund Freud, *The Ego and the Id*, trans. Riviere (New York: Norton, 1962), 31.

56. Pierre Teilhard de Chardin, *Human Energy*, trans. J. M. Cohen (New York: Harcourt Brace Jovanovich, 1962), 33.

57. Mt 5:44, Lk 6:27, 6:35.

out paradoxically that it is equivalent to hellfire for those who are not willing to receive it.[58]

For someone who wants to know "what God is like," many conjectures and stereotypes are available. Like the prophet Elias, who looked for God in the wind, an earthquake, and fire, before finally deciding he had found God in a faint whisper,[59] we would do well to look beyond depictions of God that emphasize power and might, keeping in mind that the power of love is the force apparently most basic to divine operations in the world. If God's "distinguishing characteristic" is simply the highest degree of love (*agapê*, "charity" in some translations of the Bible), most likely and logically we might do well to look for God in the traces of divine love received from or given to fellow humans and God, as far as these are detectable in our environment. God in the New Testament is referred to as "Father." Unlike the rule of a master over slaves or minions, the rule of a good father is characterized by love, and building up an atmosphere of love, albeit not excluding instances of discipline and punishment.

58. Rom 12:20.
59. 1 Kgs 19:11–13.

4
Faith

We walk by faith, not by sight.

—2 Corinthians 5:7

When the Son of Man comes, will he find faith on earth?

—Luke 18:8

COMMON MEANINGS

"FAITH" IS OFTEN EQUATED WITH "BELIEF," ALTHOUGH THE TWO TERMS are by no means synonymous. Belief is often characterized as a murky, incomplete approximation to knowledge, based on greater or lesser evidence, and often erroneous. Except for those for whom "seeing is believing," belief always falls short of knowledge, although the stereotypical believer may grit his or her teeth and hold on to some specific conviction as if it was a matter of certain knowledge. Many critics of religion direct their criticisms at faith in the sense of "belief," arguing that the beliefs that are held are a subjective state, the result of mere conformity to tradition, habit, superstition, fears of social ostracism, fears of eternal punishment, etc. They contrast this state of belief with the relative certainty that can be attained, for example, by the positive verification of a hypothesis in science. If a scientist believes a certain reaction will take place under certain conditions, and attains the necessary experimental verification, a validation of the belief is attained, a state that can allegedly not be attained by any religious belief.

But faith is not necessarily synonymous with belief as an intermediary state, and is not necessarily opposed to knowledge. There is a natural faith, for instance, that is a prerequisite for knowledge. This is the presupposition that things are indeed intelligible; or, for some ambitious minds, it may even be a wholesale, enthusiastic confidence in the intelligibility of the world. This faith is more accurately described as an *a priori* type of knowledge, a *knowing that we can know*, which impels us to the thought processes issuing in knowledge. The Hindu *Upanishads* seem to recognize the interrelationship between faith, thinking, and knowledge, in stating:

> When a man thinks, then he can know. He who does not think, does not know: know the nature of thought. When a man has faith then he thinks. He who has not faith does not think: know the nature of faith.[1]

"Faith in oneself" is also no mere belief, but a psychological characteristic frequently promoted in modern American culture: a sense of confidence, usually nurtured by social support, and by a pattern of successes—assurance that one has the ability to attain certain goals. It can be a prerequisite for the attainment of difficult objectives and the overcoming of obstacles. It depends, of course, on one's "level of aspiration." A person who has goals that are easily attainable with minimum exertion needs little of this faith. But someone with challenging goals who has this type of faith may go beyond belief to a species of certain knowledge about what he or she can do or become.

"Faith in others," or "faith in humanity," is no mere tentative speculation about a possibility, but a firm confidence in the inherent goodness of most people, and/or our ability to tap into that goodness and/or benefit from it. According to some behavioral geneticists, liberals tend to acquire this characteristic more easily than conservatives, who tend to be wary of the twists and turns of human nature, and prioritize rules and tradition.[2]

The belief in the existence of God, which a person may arrive at after a process of rational investigation of arguments, may be a springboard to religious faith, but does not necessarily lead to faith in God.

RELIGIOUS FAITH

Faith, as Construed in Major Ancient Eastern Religions

Buddhism is sometimes referred to as a "religion," but if religion entails a commitment to God or some supreme being, Buddhism is cer-

---

1. *The Upanishads*, trans. Juan Mascaró (Baltimore: Penguin Books, 1973), 119.

2. Nicholas Pastore's *The Nature-Nurture Controversy* (New York: King's Crown Press, 1949) is a classic study of this interrelationship; Stephen Pinker's *The Blank Slate: The Modern Denial of Human Nature* (New York: Viking, 2003), 283 ff. discusses recent studies concerning genetic bases for liberal and conservative political attitudes.

tainly not a religion. The efforts of Buddhists through exercises of meditation and right living to follow in the path of the Buddha (Siddhartha Gautama, born about 563 B.C.), should not be interpreted as attempts at attaining union with a divinity. The Buddha claimed no divinity or divine calling, but claimed only to be a teacher for attaining a high state of perfection, called Enlightenment. The Buddhist *sutras* and other writings are not "scriptures" in the sense of the sacred writings of Judaism, Christianity, or Islam, but rather guidebooks for the attainment of a spiritual state of *Nirvana,* which in this life will have the side effects of enhancing freedom and mitigating subjection to suffering.

Hinduism is more clearly a religion, although it is not traceable to any revered founder, and its sacred books are not considered to be the revealed Word of God. Some see the cultural and psychological aspects of Hinduism as its essential aspects. For example, Transcendental Meditation, widely practiced in the West, is primarily a cultural export, although it has some earmarks of religious ritual, such as the "mantra" entrusted to proficients in mediation techniques. But Hinduism includes belief in a supreme being, similar to the idea of God in monotheistic religions, although incorporating elements of polytheism, since (according to the most liberal interpretations) the supreme deity, Brahman, takes on various forms such as the gods Shiva, Krishna, etc. Faith for a proficient Hindu is highly experiential, involving the attainment through meditative and ascetic practices, and right living, of a state of transcendence beyond reason, but not conflicting with rationality. Belief in eternal life or reincarnation after death is also common in Hinduism.

Faith, as Construed in Judaism

The references to faith as a personal virtue or quality in the Hebrew Scriptures are few and far between,[3] but there are many references to "fidelity" and "faithfulness," indicating that "faith," for the Israelites and the Jews who remained after the North/South split of the Hebrew tribes, connoted a kind of contractual good faith, a reciprocal faithfulness to the terms of the covenant that had been enacted between Yahweh and the chosen representatives of the Hebrews. Individual faithfulness to the commandments and ritual laws laid down in the Pentateuch was also an essential aspect of Jewish faith. The

---

3. Exceptions include Prv 15:27 and Is 11:5.

great twelfth-century rabbi Maimonides enumerated the essential aspects of faith in his treatise on the *Thirteen Principles*. The thirteen articles of Jewish faith, according to Maimonides, are (1) the existence of the Creator; (2) the unique oneness of God; (3) God's incorporeality; (4) the absolute precedence of God to everything; (5) only God should be worshipped; (6) God's prophets are worthy of belief; (7) Moses has precedence among the prophets; (8) Moses received the Torah from heaven; (9) the Torah cannot be added to or subtracted from; (10) the providence of God in human affairs; (11) God rewards the good and punishes the wicked in the world to come; (12) the Messiah, descended from the seed of Solomon, will come; and (13) the righteous of the nations will rise from the dead.[4] Against the currently widespread "received opinion" that belief in life after death and resurrection is a specifically Christian doctrine, Jon Levenson has catalogued in great detail evidence of the emergence of belief both in immortality and resurrection in Hebrew scriptures and traditions.[5]

Faith in Christianity

Among Christians,[6] we find a differential emphasis on the subjective and the objective aspects of faith. Catholicism, Orthodoxy, and "High Church" Anglicanism emphasize the objective aspects, as exemplified in the Apostles' Creed, the Nicene Creed, the Athanasian Creed,

---

4. See David R. Blumenthal, *The Commentary of R. Hoter ben Shelomo to the Thirteen Principles of Maimonides* (Leiden: E. J. Brill, 1974).

5. Jon Levenson, *Resurrection and the Restoration of Israel: The Ultimate Victory of the God of Life* (New Haven, Conn.: Yale University Press, 2006) and *Resurrection: the Power of God for Christians and Jews,* by Levenson and Kevin Manning (New Haven, Conn.: Yale University Press, 2008); see also Frank Tipler's analysis of development of concepts of immortality and resurrection in the Tamud in *The Physics of Immortality: Modern Cosmology, God and the Resurrection of the Dead* (New York: Doubleday, 1994), 285–90.

6. William Lad Sessions in *The Concept of Faith: A Philosophical Investigation* (Ithaca: Cornell University Press, 1994) develops six "models" of faith, categorized according to the subjective aspects of the believer, and, if objects are involved, whether the object is personal or impersonal, present or future, real or ideal, etc. These models cluster together to a greater or lesser extent, showing some "family resemblances." But they are structures that can be associated with a variety of content, religious or nonreligious. In Christianity, Sessions differentiates a Catholic/Thomistic conception of faith that features two of his models—an orientation to objective doctrines and a personal relationship with God and Christ—from the Lutheran conception, which emphasizes the model of personal relationship, and also the models of subjective devotion and the attitude of proactive volition. These models help to capture some of the denominational aspects prevalent in contemporary Christianity, but, as we shall see in what follows, these and other conceptions of faith in Christian denominations seem to omit many of the aspects connected with faith in the New Testament.

and doctrinal pronouncements by church leaders. The focus is on the intellectual acceptance of supernaturally revealed truths[7]—for example, the Trinitarian nature of God, the Incarnation, the Virgin Birth, the Redemption by Jesus Christ, the death and resurrection of Christ, the governance of the Church with the assistance of the Holy Spirit, the bodily resurrection of the dead and future existence after death. Christians of Orthodox denominations are similar to Catholics in their emphasis on tradition and doctrine, but with a special focus on a mystical encounter with the divine, less utilization of philosophical approaches, and differences regarding dogmatic definitions, including the long-standing debate about whether the Holy Spirit proceeds both from the Father and from the Son.

In mainstream Protestantism, the notion of faith is often related to Scripture, sometimes literally interpreted; and is construed primarily as a cooperative act of the human will, committing itself unconditionally to grace and forgiveness from God through Christ, rather than an act of the intellect assenting to certain truths or "mysteries." Thus Martin Luther, criticizing what he considered to be the common Roman Catholic interpretation of faith as a general belief in truths about Christ, but without personal assimilation, writes:

> That alone can be called Christian faith, which believes without wavering that Christ is the Saviour not only to Peter and to the saints but also to you. Your salvation does not depend on the fact that you believe Christ to be the Saviour of the godly, but that he is a Saviour to you and has become your own.[8]

Faith as a gift of grace, enabling a person to remain in a personal relationship with Jesus as savior, is the source of justification and salvation for the Christian, as interpreted by Luther, and by Protestantism in general. This was contrasted with the Catholic approach to faith and justification, which, according to a frequent Protestant construal, emphasized good works rather than freely offered grace.

Since the mid-sixties, numerous ecumenical dialogues have taken place between Catholics and Protestants. Mark Noll and Carolyn Nystrom document meetings of Roman Catholics with Anglicans from

---

7. On the nature of faith as an intellectual acceptance of revealed truths, see St. Thomas Aquinas, *Summa theologiae* I-II, q. 56, 3c; II-II q. 1, 4c; q. 2, 9; q. 4, 1c.

8. *Sermons of Martin Luther: The Church Postils* (Grand Rapids, Mich.; Baker Books, 1996), vol. 1, 21.

1966 through 1996, with Methodists from 1967 through 1996, with Reformed churches from 1970 through 1990, with Lutherans from 1972
through 1999, with Disciples of Christ from 1977 through 1993, with
Evangelicals from 1977 through 1984, and with Baptists from 1984
through 1988;[9] and also the four joint statements issued by the Evangelicals and Catholics Together (ETC) group since 1994.[10] But of special interest is the Joint Declaration concerning justification by faith,
signed on Reformation Day, Oct. 31, 1999, after decades of meetings
between Catholic and Lutheran theologians[11]—since the theological
issue concerning the relative importance of faith and works for justification had been a major obstacle to hopes of reunification of Catholicism and Protestantism for six centuries. The Joint Declaration satisfies
the requirements of both parties, but has not yet been accepted widely
throughout Protestant denominations. Faith, as defined in the Joint
Declaration, is a freely given grace, bringing about forgiveness of sin,
making possible one's participation in the spirit of Christ, leading
through charity to good works, and preparing the soul for salvation.[12]

MULTIPLE MEANINGS OF FAITH IN CHRISTIANITY

In examining the New Testament, we can find some solid grounds for
the sense of faith elaborated in the above-mentioned Joint Declaration; specific passages from the Gospels or Epistles will resonate with
the Declaration. However, such specific passages are in the minority.
Numerous references to faith in the New Testament go widely *beyond*
either the traditional Catholic understanding that faith is an intellectual assent to revealed truths, or the common Protestant position
that faith is a voluntary commitment to a personal union with Jesus,
or even the sense of the Joint Declaration concerning faith as a divine gift bringing about forgiveness and justification. I do not wish to
be a literalist or a proponent of *sola scriptura*—but it does seem worth-
while to examine more closely the many scriptural passages that do

9. See Mark A. Noll and Carolyn Nystrom, *Is the Reformation Over?* (Grand Rapids, Mich.:
Baker Academic, 2005), 77–83.

10. Ibid., 153–83.

11. Ibid., 107 ff.

12. The complete text of the Joint Declaration is available at the Vatican Web site: http://
www.vatican.va/roman_curia/pontifical_councils/chrstuni/documents/rc_pc_chrstuni_doc
31101999_cath-luth-joint-declaration_en.html.

not fit easily into the "official" formulations given in Christianity, before proceeding further in an analysis of faith. As we examine these texts, we find concepts of faith that are at least of philosophical, if not theological, interest, concerning the nature of faith, its sources, its characteristics, and its effects.

The Nature of Faith

The closest we get in all of the Bible to a definition of faith is the famous summation in the Epistle to the Hebrews: "Faith is the realization of what is hoped for, and evidence of things not seen."[13] Variations of translations of this passage occur. The Greek word that is translated as "realization" is *hypostasis* (Ψπόστασις), which is usually translated in the Bible as "substance" or "being," and some New Testament translations of this passage render the term as "substance."[14] "Realization" in English often connotes a subjective attainment of a goal, whereas "substance" brings to mind an objective grounding for something.[15] Perhaps "undergirding" or "germinal essence" would be close to Paul's meaning, as a subjective guarantee or even an objective essence of an inchoate spiritual reality that was growing into maturity.

Among theologians in the Middle Ages, there was considerable debate as to whether or not this statement in Hebrews amounted to a definition. St. Thomas Aquinas devotes a special article in his *Summa* to this question.[16] Aquinas concludes that, although the definition is not in correct syllogistic form, it amounts to what in Aristotelian terminology would be an "informal" definition. He then goes on to reformulate this passage as a more properly formal definition: "Faith is the habit of the mind, by which eternal life begins within us, causing the intellect to assent to that which has not yet appeared."[17] In this reformulation, Aquinas brings together the subjective and objective connotations of *hypostasis*—faith is a habit, or virtue, of the mind, and also the seminal implantation of eternal life; and, though oriented

13. Heb 11:1.

14. For example, in the King James and Douay-Rheims versions.

15. The debate about the proper translation of *hypostasis* still continues among Scripture scholars. See the commentary on Heb 11 by Myles Bourke in *The New Jerome Biblical Commentary*, ed. Raymond Brown et al., (Englewood Cliffs, N.J.: Prentice Hall, 1968), 939.

16. *Summa theologiae* 2–2, q. 4, a. 1.

17. "*Fides est habitus mentis, qua inchoatur vita aeterna in nobis, faciens intellectum assentire non apparentibus.*"

toward an unseen "homeland,"[18] it brings about the same type of assent or conviction that is generated by objective realities that are encountered here and now. In other words, it is the grounding in our present life for our entry into eternal life, and supplies believers with the evidence they need for the existence of a transcendent realm.

This definition is obviously paradoxical. It is experiential, but designates an experience that is not an experience in any ordinary sense. That is, it refers to an experience of being able to go beyond experience. The "substance" or substantial "realization" that the author of Hebrews refers to is, to utilize more philosophical language, a power or "potency" that complements the natural capabilities of the believer. And the paradoxical experience that results is an encounter with the "evidence" for the unseen mysteries to which faith is directed.

The Source of Faith

A Christian thinks of the Apostles and disciples after Pentecost, traveling out into the then-known world to spread the "good news." Many of them—having had contact with the Christ, seeing his works, witnessing his resurrection, receiving empowerment from the Spirit— were comparable, if a secular contrast be permissible, to a reporter who had just come upon a scoop, and was impatient to spread the news; or, perhaps more appropriately, comparable to the woman in Luke 15:8–9 who finds a lost coin she had been searching diligently for, and goes out proclaiming her good fortune to all her neighbors.

If we ask about the source of faith for these first Christians, for some of them the source may have been the fact that they took seriously the admonition of Christ to "search the Scriptures."[19] But for many of them, it is clear that the primary source was preaching, in some cases by Christ himself, or by John the Baptist.[20] St. Paul points to preaching as the ordinary source for the activation of faith:

> Whosoever shall call upon the name of the Lord shall be saved. How then shall they call on him in whom they have not believed? and how shall they believe in him whom they have not heard? and how shall they hear without a preacher?[21]

18. Heb 11:14.
19. Jn 5:39, 5:46, 7:52.
20. Mt 21:32; Mk 11:31.
21. Rom 10:13–15.

But formidable obstacles stand in the way of the efficacity of preaching, as Christ himself points out in his parable of the sower with the seed:

> The seed is the word of God. Those on the path are the ones who have heard, but the devil comes and takes away the word from their hearts that they may not believe and be saved.[22]

If preaching is not the most effective mode in some cases, what other sources are available for eliciting the faith of the believer? Christ offers one alternative source. Those who don't believe his words may be convinced by his "works"—that is, the "signs" that he offers;[23] and the disciples he is sending out to spread the announcement of the coming of the Kingdom will also be distinguished and recognized by their "signs"—casting out demons, speaking new languages, healing the sick, etc.[24] To these signs, Paul adds the gift of prophecy and the gift of tongues (the "glossalalia").[25] The signs that were almost exclusively offered by Christ himself were exorcisms of evil spirits and miraculous healings. One may presume that it was primarily signs, rather than preaching or Scripture, that elicited the faith of the Caananite woman who asked Jesus for the "leftovers" after he had accommodated the Jews,[26] and the faith of the Roman centurion who sent a messenger to ask Jesus to cure his servant.[27]

Are miraculous "signs" still given to bolster faith? Some may want to point to the occasional "private revelations" discussed in chapter 3, or miraculous healings at shrines like that in Lourdes, France, at which teams of doctors examine cases of alleged cures after people have bathed in the spring; or through the ministration of exceptional individuals such as St. Padre Pio of Pietrelcina (1910–68), by whose intercession numerous inexplicable healings were reported; or to occasional public miracles witnessed by tens of thousands—such as the miracle of the sun mentioned in chapter 3, or the apparitions of the Virgin Mary in Zeitun, Egypt, in 1968 and 1969.[28]

22. Lk 8:12. See also Mt 13:18.
23. Jn 10:38.
24. Mk 16:17.
25. 1 Cor 14:22.
26. Mt 8:10.
27. Mt 15:28; Lk 7:9.
28. See Pearl Zaki, *Before Our Eyes: The Virgin Mary, Zeitun Egypt 1968 and 1969* (Goleta, Calif.: Queenship, 2002) and the Web site, http://www.zeitun-eg.org.

Skepticism about the factuality, or even the possibility, of miracles is common now, even among Christian theologians, to whom a miracle seems an unwarranted and unnecessary intervention by God in the very laws of nature that He created. Among some believers, one may discern an element of pride that they don't "need" miracles to bolster their faith. The often unappreciated source for this view is to be found in the anti-Christian sentiment of the eighteenth-century Enlightenment. As Tipler observes, "The idea that a miracle violates the laws of physics was introduced in the English-speaking world by the Deists, whose motivation was to deny the Resurrection and the Incarnation. If a miracle violated physical law, if the Resurrection and the Incarnation violated physical law, then the Deists could use the strong evidence that physical laws were never violated as evidence against the Resurrection and Incarnation. Hume [in his treatise on miracles] just continued and expanded this Deist strategy."[29]

The possible ongoing importance of miracles in relationship to faith will be discussed in chapter 7. But in any case, signs are not a *sine qua non* for one's faith. Jesus even warned about depending too much on signs.[30]

What, then, are the major sources of faith *now*—hopefully, sources that may inspire the sort of enthusiasm reported among the first Christians? Have they changed? Theoretically, technology is so advanced now that the Gospel, as "Good News," could be proclaimed worldwide with the use of radio, satellite television, the internet, etc.

But the practical obstacles in the way of this communication seem insuperable. How can the message of the Gospel be communicated to aborigines, the illiterate, the isolated? To individuals in dictatorial regimes prohibiting free speech; to individuals in religious sects that distort and vitiate the word of God, and/or spread violent sectarian rivalries, and/or use force to prevent hearing of the Word; or to secularists surrounded by family, friends, colleagues, and a culture that has imbibed the alternative "good news" (namely, that science has all the answers, and scientific orthodoxy should be the litmus test for beliefs)? How can the Gospel be conveyed to those in progressive, industrialized societies that are just too busy to listen?

Scriptures and preaching are still major sources. But which scriptures? Protestants and Catholics have several disagreements about what is canonical in the Bible; meanings are sometimes changed dras-

---

29. Frank Tipler, *The Physics of Christianity*, 102.
30. Mt 12:39, 16:4.

tically in new translations; and Scripture scholars sometimes bracket out whole sections of the Bible as editorial additions, historically mistaken, appeals to select audiences, and so forth. Learned theologians often deny the bodily resurrection of Jesus (in spite of Paul's admonition[31] that faith would be in vain without it) and Jesus's ascension into heaven; and the notorious "Jesus seminar" casts doubt on the veracity of most of the Gospel narratives. Finally, even granted that the written *evangelium* is intact, how do we distinguish preachers who are "sent" from those who are not sent? The problem of "false prophets" will be discussed in chapter 7.

But it may be a mistake to put too much emphasis on Scriptures and preaching. Other sources may predominate for some people. For instance, the investigation of nature, if not a major source of faith, is certainly an important auxiliary source in all eras, since:

> Ever since the creation of the world, God's invisible attributes of eternal power and divinity have been able to be understood and perceived in what he has made.[32]

In the contemporary world, with the exponential growth of scientific knowledge, this source may be more important than it has ever been in the past. As St. Paul mentions, the basic prerequisite for faith is that one comes to believe that God exists, and that He rewards those who seek him;[33] and, as mentioned in Chapter 1,[34] contemplation of Nature seems to be a path to faith taken by many in the scientific community. Awareness of a Designer can be a starting point for transition to a belief in divine providence and eternal life.

But we have been discussing the various *external* sources—preaching, Scripture, "signs," evidence in nature of design. How is it that these sources can elicit or activate the response of faith? Must there not also be an *internal* source, an internal impetus, to which these sources correspond, perhaps in the same way that facts and evidence seem to be open to the searching mind of the rational investigator? Is there not some instinctive basis, necessary to explain a response of faith, adapted and adequate to supernatural and suprarational "stimuli"? This question will be considered in detail in the next chapter.

31. 1 Cor 15:14.
32. Rom 1:20.
33. Heb 11:6.
34. See above, p. 27.

The Characteristics of Faith

Faith is described by St. Paul as an indistinct vision of the divine:

> At present we see indistinctly, as in a mirror, but then face to face. At present I know partially; then I shall know fully, as I am fully known.[35]

There are a variety of "mirrors" in which we may see partial reflections of God. Signs of divinity and power and creativity can be seen in nature, as St. Paul notes,[36] unless by some strange cerebral gyrations a hyperenlightened individual perceives in nature only the incredible workings of Chance as a substitute for divinity. Since humans are made in the image of God,[37] more or less distinct visions of divine love, wisdom, and power are available in our neighbors, unless we habitually view them with the glasses of indifference or hate.[38] And a Christian who meditates on the life and deeds of Jesus will come to see evidence of divinity (as C. S. Lewis notes, to see him as just a "great ethical teacher" would be self-contradictory, because it would not be very ethical to claim falsely to be the son of God. The only viable alternative would be to see him as a lunatic).[39]

Although doubt is compatible with a search for the proper objects of faith, the indistinct vision of the divine that comes through the "mirror reflections" of faith can be free from doubt,[40] just as, while looking at a reflection of someone, we may lament the fuzziness or cloudiness of the image, but have no doubts about who is being represented.

Another characteristic of faith is an openness to divine power. There are numerous examples of this in the Gospels, in instances where those who are seeking a miraculous healing are admonished to "have faith" as a prerequisite for the healing to take place.[41] Such openness can also be a continual, habitual state, an abandonment to divine providence,[42] which manifests itself particularly at times when human assistance is out of the question, or when believers voluntar-

---

35. 1 Cor 13:12.
36. Rom 1:20.
37. Gn 1:26–27; 9:6.
38. Jn 4:20.
39. C. S. Lewis, *Mere Christianity* (New York: Macmillan, 1952), 41.
40. Jas 1:6. "If any of you lacks wisdom, he should ask God. . . . Ask in faith, not doubting, for the one who doubts is like a wave of the sea that is driven and tossed about by the wind."
41. See, for example, Mt 9:2, 9:22, 9:29; Mk 5:34, 9:23–24, 10:52; Lk 8:48, 8:50, 17:19, 18:42; Acts 3:16, 14:9; Jas 5:14–15.
42. Mt 6:30, 16:8.

ily divest themselves from ordinary sustenance. The Yogi Paramahansa Yogananda, in his autobiography, describes a stage in his development when he and a companion, with the support of their spiritual director, undertook a journey with no money and without begging, to solidify their faith in divine providence.[43] As a somewhat similar test of faith, students preparing for the Catholic priesthood in the Jesuit Order will often be sent to travel without funding, depending on the kindness of strangers or opportunities for employment that come their way.

Besides such passive openness to God's power, faith may take the form of an openness to participating actively in manifestations of divine power. The most dramatic reference to this is the rather stunning assurance Jesus offers to his followers:

> Amen, I say to you, if you have faith the size of a mustard seed, you will say to this mountain, "Move from here to there," and it will move. Nothing will be impossible for you.[44]

Commentators on Scripture from the earliest times have almost always taken this as metaphorical, as a reference to the great things that can be accomplished in God's service, depending on the degree of one's faith. But in the Orthodox Christian tradition, there are instances in which the saying was taken literally. A fourth-century Orthodox saint, Venerable Mark the Anchorite of Athens, is reputed to have moved a mountain into the sea. And in the Egyptian Coptic Orthodox hagiography, Saint Simon the Tanner in the tenth-century, taunted by a challenge from the Muslim Caliph Al Muizz, is said to have moved the Mokattam Mountain as testimony to the superiority of Christianity over Islam. Needless to say, if such powerful manifestations of faith were available in our day, the choice of a religion for some seekers would be unproblematic.

Finally, faith is manifested actively in courageous perseverance in the face of death and against the forces of evil, as exemplified in Jesus's words to Simon Peter:

> Simon, Simon, behold Satan has demanded to sift all of you like wheat, but I have prayed that your own faith may not fail; and once you have turned back, you must strengthen your brothers.[45]

43. See *Autobiography of a Yogi* (London: Rider & Co., 1969), chap. 11.
44. Mt 17:20. See also Mt 21:21; Mk 11:22; Lk 17:5.
45. Lk 22:32. See also 1 Cor. 16:13; Eph 6:16; Heb 11:32–34; Mk 5:36; Mt 14:31.

The ultimate manifestation of the strengthening caused by faith is, of course, the unflinching courage and patience of martyrs enduring extraordinary sufferings at the hands of opponents of the faith.

The Effects of Faith

Once a person's life has been transformed by faith, the manifestation of that transformation is by no means uniform. As St. Paul points out,[46] faith is measured out, or apportioned, in various ways to various participants. He mentions seven specific ways that faith is manifested, diverse modes that converge to produce an organic unity in the "spiritual body" of Christ:[47] (1) prophetic or charismatic preaching, (2) ministries of service, (3) ministries of teaching, (4) ministries of counseling or exhortation, (5) ministries of philanthropy, (6) ministries of leadership or administration, and (7) ministries of mercy. This enumeration of the gifts of faith is not, of course, meant to indicate a sharp "division of labor" among believers, but only to specify the ways in which some believers will excel according to the "measure" of their faith, while not necessarily excluding their possession of other gifts to various degrees.

Besides this enumeration of the variety of gifts that are bestowed by faith, Paul also refers to faith in some places as a unique, special gift of the Spirit, which differentiates and signalizes some Christians, and either goes beyond the usual meaning of faith, or designates an extraordinary intensity of faith. Thus he writes:

> To one is given through the Spirit the expression of wisdom; to another the expression of knowledge according to the same Spirit; to another faith by the same Spirit; to another gifts of healing.[48]

and

> If I have the gift of prophecy and comprehend all mysteries and all knowledge; if I have all faith so as to move mountains but do not have love, I am nothing.[49]

46. Rom 12:3.
47. Rom 12:6–8.
48. 1 Cor 12:8–9.
49. 1 Cor 13:2.

The person of "faith" envisioned in such passages seems to be not just one who believes, or even believes strongly, but one for whom "everything is possible,"[50] if not specifically the "moving of mountains." In other words, this is the person who accomplishes, through faith, things that by common consensus are considered to be impossible even by fellow "faithful" Christians.

One final effect of faith is the creation of unity in the Mystical Body of Christ:

> He gave some as apostles, others as prophets, others as evangelists, others as pastors and teachers, to equip the holy ones for the work of ministry, for building up the body of Christ, until we all attain to the unity of faith and knowledge of the Son of God, to mature manhood, to the extent of the full stature of Christ.[51]

Amid the tremendous variety of gifts and offices and ministries in the Church, it is faith that brings about the unity necessary for their harmonious coordination and collaboration in a quasi-organic manner. Without the unity of faith, these segments are like the dry bones in the desert that Ezekiel speaks of,[52] unable to be inserted into the proper sockets, take on flesh, and become a living body.

Needless to say, the varied characteristics and effects of faith just considered do not fit neatly into the conventional Catholic or Protestant definitions of faith. They go considerably beyond both the notion of faith as an intellectual assent to revealed truths or as a personal, trusting relationship to Christ. But some commonality can be pointed out. Christian faith in its multiple manifestations has to do with transcendent aspects interconnected with the "normal" or the "natural"— in human thinking, experiences, relationships, aspirations, potentialities, and behavior. If human nature in some way rises to that which transcends nature, how can this be explained? Is there some important intrinsic connection between the immanent and the transcendent, the natural and the supernatural? The theory of a faith-instinct considered in the next chapter points in that direction.

---

50. Mk 9:23.
51. Eph 4:11–13.
52. Ez 37:1–114.

5

The Faith-Instinct

He who believes has a sufficient inducement to believe: for he is
led to belief by an interior instinct of God inviting him.
　　　　—Thomas Aquinas, *Summa theologiae* II-II, q. 2, a. 9.

Deep in human nature (and so in every man) the image of God
is imprinted, that is, a quality that constitutes in it—and even without it—a kind of secret call to the object of the full and supernatural revelation brought by Christ.
　　　　—Henri de Lubac, *The Church—Paradox and Mystery*.

"There is within the human mind, and indeed by natural instinct,
an awareness of divinity." This we take to be beyond controversy.
To prevent anyone from taking refuge in the pretense of ignorance, God himself implanted in all men a certain understanding
of his divine majesty. . . . This conviction, namely, that there is
some God, is naturally inborn in all, and is fixed deep within, as
it were in the very marrow.
　　　　—John Calvin, *Institutes of the Christian Religion*, I, iii.

THE PROBLEM OF HUMAN INSTINCTS

IT IS COMMONLY THOUGHT THAT HUMANS ARE RELATIVELY FREE OF
instincts, and thus superior to animals, who are ruled completely or
almost completely by instinct, and have, at the most, only faint ap-
proximations to human thought. We admit, of course, that simple instincts like sucking, for newborn babies, and the sex instinct, emerge
in the course of development, activated by appropriate stimuli. Some
will go deeper into ethology, and assert that there is in humans terri-
toriality, or something very similar to the jealous "territoriality-drives"
of animals; possibly also defensive mechanisms, competition for mates
and prestige, and an altruism similar to the occasional sacrifices of

animals for conspecifics. But these characteristics are more often characterized as "drives" or "tendencies," rather than instincts. Some of the more assertive and controversial theorists have pointed out major areas in which humans are allegedly ruled by instincts purely and simply—that is, patterns of behavior or thinking that are unlearned, passed on from generation to generation. Examples of this include Noam Chomsky's theory that a "universal grammar" for all language is not a learned acquisition but an instinctive endowment, and Carl Jung's theory that the human unconscious is endowed at birth with certain universal archetypes, which tend to shape the way individuals perceive authority figures, the sexes, their own personal integrations, etc. Such theories are held by only a minority, but seem to throw light on some questions about human characteristics and behavior.[1]

Could faith itself be the result of instinct? Recent work by scientists has suggested a possible biological basis for religion—the possible connection between neural circuits in the brain, or genetics, and religious experience. For example, Francis Collins, in *The Language of God*,[2] and Andrew Newberg in *Why God Won't Go Away*,[3] see the "need for God" as implanted in the structure of the brain. Barbara Bradley Hagerty in *Fingerprints of God: The Search for the Science of Spirituality*,[4] in numerous interviews with neuroscientists, researchers of identical twins, geneticists, and other scientists, uncovers evidence that an orientation toward spiritual transcendence is "hardwired" into the brain. Henry Rosemont, an atheist, and Huston Smith, a theist, in a recent dialogue,[5] agree on the existence of a religious instinct analogous to the "universal grammar" theorized by Noam Chomsky, although they disagree about its ontological implications (that is, whether it offers any evidence of a transnatural reality). Numerous other works trace religious experiences or orientations to biological sources.[6]

If these hypotheses were validated, we would merely have further evidence of a physical trigger for what Freud called the "oceanic ex-

---

1. For an extensive discussion of these possibilities see my *Philosophy of Human Nature* (Chicago: Open Court, 2008), chap. 2.

2. New York: Free Press, 2006.

3. New York: Ballantine, 2001.

4. New York: Riverhead Books, 2009.

5. *Is There a Universal Grammar of Religion?* (Chicago: Open Court, 2008).

6. See, for example, Eugene G. d'Aquili and Andrew B. Newberg, *The Mystical Mind: Probing the Biology of Religious Experience* (Minneapolis: Fortress Press, 1999); Ian Barbour, *Nature, Human Nature, and God* (Minneapolis: Fortress, 2002); and Dean Hamer, *The God Gene: How Faith is Hardwired into our Genes* (New York: Doubleday, 2004).

perience"—a peak experience in which an individual feels at one with the cosmos, and which may or may not have religious connotations for that individual. But if faith is a quality or virtue of the rational soul, and consonant with human freedom, something more than genetic predispositions or neurologically initiated feelings or sentiments would be needed to give it authenticity. In the human soul, a "faith-instinct" would have to be intimately associated with the thinking and willing peculiar to human beings, and go far beyond physically conditioned feelings or desires, which may be completely absent.

The Tübingen theologian, Max Seckler, finds some interesting substantiations regarding the instinctive nature of faith in the writings of Thomas Aquinas. In his book, *Instinkt und Glaubenswille nach Thomas von Aquin* ("Instinct and the Will to Believe, According to Thomas Aquinas"),[7] he follows the development of this leading idea in Aquinas, analyzes its sources, and offers an interpretation relevant to current theological currents. The present chapter is indebted to Seckler's exposition. In the final two chapters, the wider implications of the concept of a faith-instinct (*Glaubensinstinkt*) will be discussed.

PHILOSOPHICAL UNDERPINNINGS FOR THE CONCEPT OF A FAITH-INSTINCT

Segments of the *Eudemian Ethics*[8] of Aristotle and the pseudo-Aristotelian *Magna moralia*[9] came out in a medieval work, *Liber de bona fortuna*, translated from the Greek either by Bartholomaeus of Messina or Robert Grosseteste. Thomas Aquinas's acquaintance with the *Eudemian Ethics* was only through the *Liber de bona fortuna*, since he did not have direct access to the original Aristotelian or pseudo-Aristotelian works. In general, the *Liber de bona fortuna* ("Treatise Concerning Good Fortune") has to do with the nature of luck and its relationship to happiness. But in the course of the analysis of luck, the question emerges: Is the element that activates human *thought* and endeavors possibly a matter of luck? This leads in the Treatise to a citation of Aristotle's response, which is: "Just as God exists in the entire universe, so also in us. It is the divine within that moves us."[10]

---

7. Mainz: Matthias-Grünewald-Verlag, 1961.
8. VII, 14 (1246, b37–1248, b11).
9. II, 8 (1206, b30–1207, b19).
10. Max Seckler, *op. cit.* p. 107. Hereafter cited as Seckler. Seckler footnotes, and translates

Aquinas interpreted this Aristotelian response to mean that the principle of actuality in the soul is something that, going beyond mere "luck," is much "better" than human reason—namely, God, who is the principle of every movement.[11] This notion, of a divine within the human, seemed to offer to Aquinas a possible solution concerning the ontological grounding for the psychological aspects of faith discussed by Augustine, as we shall see below.

According to Seckler, elements of Stoic philosophy also entered into Aquinas's approach. Just as, for the Stoics, "Nature" had the double aspect—an active cosmic *Nous,* and also human reason actively participating in this *Nous*—so also, for Aquinas, "Nature" connoted both the ordering of the totality, and the existential determinacy of the rational individual participating in the order of nature.[12]

Seckler suggests that writings of the Spanish philosopher Isador of Seville (560–635), who was influenced by the ethics and philosophy of law of the Stoics, gave an additional impetus to Aquinas to look for an individuated grounding in the soul for the emergence of faith:

> [According to the *Etymologies* of Isador of Seville,] God's action, to which the creature is necessarily subordinated, is transmitted according to distinctive laws in each nature, and indeed brings it about that everything that God can and will require from his creature corresponds to some tendency and yearning in the creature.[13]

THE AUGUSTINIAN THEOLOGICAL UNDERPINNING

St. Augustine, in resolute opposition to the Pelagian heresy, which portrayed faith as a "do it yourself" accomplishment of human free will, with divine grace as a supplemental, epiphenomenal support, maintained that, in addition to extrinsic instigations to faith such as

---

from, the original Greek, and gives the Latin version in an appendix. In Aristotle's *Eudemian Ethics,* Book 7, chapter 14, the segment in question reads, "What is the commencement of movement in the soul? The answer is clear: as in the universe, so in the soul, it is god. For in a sense the divine element in us moves everything. The starting-point of reasoning is not reasoning, but something greater."

11. See *S. T.* I-II q. 109, a. 2, ad 1: "It is necessary that the movement of human free will finally be traced back to some exterior principle that transcends the human mind—in other words, to God." See also *Contra gentiles* III, 89.

12. Seckler, 133.

13. Ibid., 264.

the preaching of the Gospel, God also influenced the will *intrinsecus, ubi nemo habet in potestate quid ei veniat in mentem* ("intrinsically, at the level where no one has any control over what enters into his mind"). Thus Augustine maintained, contrary to Pelagius (ca. 360–420), that an internal impetus from God was the initial instigation, a prompting to which the free will of the individual could assent or withhold assent. Augustine did not use the word "instinct" to describe this impetus because of the associations the word "instinct" had in his time with astrology and the occult.[14]

But Aquinas did not have such disincentives and seemed to attach the word "instinct" to the sort of promptings that Augustine refers to. And after he became aware of the issues of semi-Pelagianism in his own time, he began to use the term "instinct" consistently in connection with the inner origins of faith:.

> [Aquinas] constantly asserted the necessity of an inner assistance as preparation for justification. He then resolutely gives this assistance the name, "instinct," especially in connection with his dogmatic psychology of faith, where this instinct is presented as the uniquely necessary, sufficient, and efficacious motive force (*inductivum*) to faith.[15]

THE FAITH-INSTINCT: THE THOMISTIC VIEW

Anthropologists often turn up evidence of religious beliefs and rituals in "primitive" peoples. These are possibly laden with superstition —but, even if superstitious, we might wonder about the psychological causes of such phenomena. According to Aquinas, humans are naturally religious; even "natural man" after Adam and Eve, prior to the advent of Abraham or Moses and Talmudic laws, possessed an instinct for worship, a deeply seated, imperious, ontological aspect of human nature itself. According to Seckler:

> Thomas recognizes a natural instinct that instills the obligation of divine worship: "Man apprehends by a certain natural instinct that he is obligated to offer in his own way worship to God, the source of his existence and of all good (III *Contra Gentiles*, 119). . . . In the state of natural law, without any external law being given, men were motivated to worship God

14. Ibid., 94.
15. Ibid., 98.

(*Summa* III 60, 5 ad 3)." The religious instinct is a legitimate and necessary tendency of nature, and the same laws prevail for it as for all norms of nature: It is an ontological law, a tendency of rational nature, which precedes all deliberation, precepts and contracts; it is and must be imposed as the norm of conscious ethical action.[16]

According to Aquinas, external inducements to faith, no matter how potent, are characteristically coordinated with an interior motive power, when the human soul is making the transition to faith:

Not only does the exterior revelation, as the object of faith, possess an attractive power, but *also an interior instinct,* impelling and leading to belief, has this power; thus the Father draws many to the Son *through the instinct of divine operation* moving the interior heart of man to belief.[17]

Only when this internal impetus is coordinated with suitable external inducements does one have the sufficient prerequisites for making the "leap" to faith.[18]

When the encounter of the inner instinct with the object of assent takes place, what results is metaphorically described as an "inner light"—"a kind of light—the habit of faith—divinely imparted to the human mind."[19] This light, according to Aquinas:

Makes us see what we believe. For just as, by the habits of the other virtues, man sees what is becoming to him in respect of that habit, so, by the habit of faith, the human mind is directed to assent to such things as are becoming to a right faith, and not to assent to others.[20]

In other words, just as the virtue of temperance will lead the temperate person to see objects of pleasure such as food and drink in a different light than the intemperate person, or the virtue of justice will lead the just person to view the exchange of goods and money in a different way than the unjust person, so also the virtue of faith will throw a different light, compared to the non-believer, on one's life in the broader sense—the goals, the means of achieving the goals, and the types of association with others that will be most conducive to attaining them.

16. Ibid., 226–27.
17. Aquinas, *In Joannem* 6, 5. Italics added.
18. *S. T.* II-II 2, 9, ad 3.
19. Aquinas, Commentary on Boethius's *De trinitate* q. 3, a. 1.
20. *S. T.* II-II q. 1, a. 4, ad 3.

ONTOLOGICAL IMPLICATIONS OF THE FAITH-INSTINCT

The instinct that leads to faith is not to be understood as a psychological disposition affecting the emotions, nor a "faith prefacing faith" (as if believing in faith could bring faith about); nor is it to be simply identified with faith that is actually willed.[21] Neither is the will to believe a consequence brought about by some actual grace, or some truth to which intellectual assent is given.[22] Rather, it is the ontological basis that must be presupposed to explain the response to the external call to faith:

> The message of Scripture, that "breathes forth love," and that fires up the secret, often unconscious, wishes of men—and thus, in this way, operates psychologically as the values discovered and recognized in the Gospel activate the will's impulses—this "Word" of external revelation would be spoken in vain, if God did not bestow the inner instinct, which out of one's interior provides the "correspondence" to the Gospel, so that this Gospel can touch the heart effectively.[23]

The faith-instinct, as a philosophical/anthropological "power of believing," belongs to the very structure of man's spiritual nature.[24] In Aquinas's formulation, it functions as the ontological basis empowering humans to believe:

> The point of origin for the religious in general is rooted in being. That which in our day is called the starting point of the religious is situated by Thomas Aquinas in the very substance of the soul.[25]

THE FORM AND CONTENT OF FAITH

The faith-instinct, like the three fundamental human inclinations described by Aquinas (self-preservation, sexual congress, and exercise of reason),[26] is completely indeterminate. "Psychologically speaking, the instincts are intrinsically without light. They are indeterminate as to content. . . . Just as a human being initially is a *blank tablet* in regard

---

21. Seckler, 103.
22. Ibid., 267.
23. Ibid., p. 103.
24. Ibid., 45.
25. Ibid., 267.
26. *S. T.* I-II q. 94, a. 2. Discussed by Seckler, 152.

to determinations, the same holds for his instincts,"[27] including the faith-instinct. Thus the faith-instinct must be "in-formed" from the environment in which it is situated:

> *Fides ex auditu* ["faith comes from hearing"]. Without the "information" coming from without, the act of faith cannot be elicited. Someone is "informed" about God's salvific action, about the status of man in God's sight, about the efficacious silent working of God's grace, about the condition of the state of grace—and what is heard and understood now "informs" the inner man, forms the faith-instinct, and objectifies the unknown and unexpected plenitude of inner grace. . . . To have faith does not mean to follow one's unclear religious instinct, but rather to see and objectify this instinct—and at the same time one's self—in the light of revelation. The faith-instinct enlightened in this way is objective faith.[28]

The relationship between the form and content of faith is thus paradoxical. The faith-instinct is a tendency that follows upon the substantial "form" of man—that is, human nature. But this tendency is a content that, as it evolves in response to external factors, takes on the form of that which it receives—that is, the objects of faith. Thus, from one point of view, the objects of faith become a content subsumed into the form of the individual soul of the believer; from another point of view, the objects of faith give form to the indeterminacies of faith that they complement:

> The basic principle [of Aquinas and the Scholastics] that *intellectus caret omnibus illis quas natus est intelligere* ["the intellect inherently lacks all that it is oriented to know"] applies also to faith. The dispensation of the grace of faith connotes a formal openness for a specific area of reality—and nothing more! This instinct in the encounter with the object of faith is transferred out of its relative initial indeterminacy and determined. It becomes more determinate, since it is formed.[29]

The in-formation that takes place, however, involves the shaping of a tendency that is already present, and thus should not be understood as merely a strong emotional movement or deliberate assent to some dogmatic belief.[30] Faith as a spiritual tendency begins to take on the

27. Seckler, 152.
28. Ibid., 154.
29. Ibid., 153.
30. Ibid., 155.

form of the objective Word, "understood by hearing, and recognized as a value."[31]

THEOLOGICAL IMPORTANCE OF THE FAITH-INSTINCT

"Faith comes through hearing," according to St. Paul;[32] and much effort in systematic theology is expended in trying to clarify when this "hearing" takes place, what forms it takes, the various objects of faith that are "heard," etc. It is generally presupposed that "hearers of the Word" must have the proper dispositions to make the transition to belief, but this, says Seckler, is something more than a psychological readiness:

> Faith comes from hearing. But the fact that hearing can and will take place, is an effect of the faith-instinct; since this disposes man interiorly for Revelation: It makes possible the hearing of the Word, fires up the desire for salvation, produces needs and confirms the fulfillment of these needs as something present at hand.[33]

More fundamental than any psychological disposition is the initial movement of the will that makes possible the acceptance of the "word" of external revelation, the inner "correspondence" to the Gospel. And this requires the direct intervention of God, insofar as He creates the moving principle of the will and "activates" faith in the will.[34]

Seckler compares the faith-instinct with other altruistic human instincts and theorizes that the faith-instinct must be an endowment of human nature itself, and thus universal:

> Someone out of a natural instinct will go to help a man who is in need. A rational instinct likewise gives us the obligation for divine worship. It is a positive disposition for grace. Even before the Mosaic law was given, prophetic men existed who, drawing on a divine instinct, created certain forms of worship; and it is valid to generalize that men situated outside the realm of revelation (i.e., in the "state of nature") were aroused through an inner instinct to reverence for God and to the development of certain forms of worship.[35]

31. Ibid., 156.
32. Rom 10:17.
33. Seckler, 264.
34. Ibid., 101, 103.
35. Ibid., 63.

In other words, humans are created with a *divine instinct,* which becomes an *instinct for the divine,*[36] and even makes theology possible and meaningful. This instinct was operative in those who existed before Moses or Abraham and is still operative in those who exist at present outside the parameters of the Judeo-Christian revelation. This alleged universality of the faith-instinct will, of course, indicate some extensions of traditional theology to ecumenism. Possible ecumenical implications will be discussed in Chapter 7.

EMPIRICAL ASPECTS OF THE FAITH-INSTINCT

In 1969, the sociologist Peter Berger published *A Rumor of Angels: Modern Society and the Rediscovery of the Supernatural,*[37] which became an unexpected best seller. With this book, written in the era of the "death of God" movement, he broke ranks with the "received wisdom" of the social sciences—that is, in avoiding any reference to the supernatural. With the eyes and technique of a sociologist, he considered areas of the culture and everyday life that gave some evidence that the supernatural had not become debilitated in secular culture but was indeed "alive and well." He focused on five "signals of transcendence": (1) *Assurances of order.* For example, a mother calming her child in the dark points to an ultimate rescue from death and chaos; or should we suppose that the mother willfully lies to the child to make him feel good? Is it a lie to say confidently that "everything will be all right"? (2) The experience of *joy in play.* He cites Nietzsche, who says, "All play wills eternity," and poses the rhetorical question: Isn't the delight of play a commonly shared experience of transcending time and our finitude? (3) *Hope,* as a continual horizon. He cites the existentialism of Gabriel Marcel, which emphasized "ultimate hope," and the revisionist Marxism of Ernst Block, who interjected the officially unorthodox idea of transcendence into mainstream Marxist materialism. (4) The *judgement of damnation* (not merely "punishment") for perpetrators of extreme inhumanity. An example uppermost in the minds of many at the time Berger wrote was the trial of Holocaust mastermind Adolph Eichmann in Israel; in our own time, a comparable example might be the 2005 suicide subway

---

36. Ibid., 114.

37. Peter Berger, *A Rumor of Angels: Modern Society and the Rediscovery of the Supernatural* (Garden City, N.Y.: Doubleday, 1969).

bombers in London, whose Islamist actions even Islamic authorities deemed to be "punishable in hell." (5) Finally, *humor,* which permits humans to escape from the limitations of life, relativizing the discrepancy between ourselves and the cosmic developments in which we are caught up. He finds Cervantes's *Don Quixote,* with its romantic/religious vision of a "better world," a good example of this "escape valve."

Similarly, Max Seckler cites certain types of experience that provide phenomenological evidence of religious tendencies. These tendencies, he says, are often initially manifested in a negative or indeterminate way—as a feeling of alienation from the world, or a sense of insufficiency or lack of fulfillment, as a sharp impression of the fleetingness of time and lack of finality, or as the experience of existential anxiety, depression, restlessness, or doubt. But positive experiences, often subsequent to the negative, also come to the fore—for example, as a general commitment to the good and the true, as a feeling of awe before incomprehensible mysteries of life, as an intuitive insight into the deeper dimensions of reality, or as a generalized impetus to transcendence. Finally, he adds:

> Ethical anguish, yearning for salvation, penitential acts, religious feeling, sensitivity to the numinous, the bewilderment of the understanding confronting the incomprehensibility of being and confronting the missing links in causality—these are the modes in which the wide-ranging category of the "religious" broadens out into psychological effects.[38]

SECKLER'S CONCLUSIONS

Following Aquinas, Seckler discerns an instinct deeply rooted in human nature itself, ontologically prior even to man's rational faculties, and developing slowly and, at first almost imperceptibly, but efficaciously, toward establishing the dispositions for faith:

> The grace for Faith is situated at the root where understanding and will are still united. This grace operates for a long time before it is an object of our knowledge; it masters our shifting spiritual movements as an instinct that is planted in basic human existence, and that is enjoined on the spirit

38. Seckler, 228.

as a tendency and inner law. This instinct is, according to Thomas, the ef-
ficacious and wide-ranging inner cause of Faith and Salvation.[39]

Seckler focuses our attention on an extremely paradoxical aspect
of human nature, since, if human beings are endowed with a faith-
instinct, they will have, in effect, a natural tendency for what is *above*
nature:

> The thesis concerning the natural yearning for the supernatural brings
> out explicitly in its inner extension the paradoxical situation of man, who
> is situated at the horizon between the finite and the infinite.[40]

But, if the analogy with other instincts is appropriate, as the faith-
instinct begins to reach this "horizon," the encounter with the objects
of faith by which it is to be "determined" is of significance. What may
be a bone fide "activation" with respect to the *supernatural?* This issue
is considered in the next chapter.

39. Ibid., 261.
40. Ibid., 265.

6
Faith—Proper and Improper Objects

Paul stood up at the Areopagus and said: "You Athenians, I see that in every respect you are very religious. For as I walked around looking carefully at your shrines, I even discovered an altar inscribed, 'To an Unknown God.' What therefore you unknowingly worship, I proclaim to you."

—Acts 17:22–23

In the day-to-day trenches of adult life, there is actually no such thing as atheism. There is no such thing as not worshipping. Everybody worships. The only choice we get is what to worship. And the compelling reason for maybe choosing some sort of god or spiritual-type thing to worship—be it JC or Allah, be it YHWH or the Wiccan Mother Goddess, or the Four Noble Truths, or some inviolable set of ethical principles—is that pretty much anything else you worship will eat you alive. If you worship money and things, if they are where you tap real meaning in life, then you will never have enough, never feel you have enough. It's the truth. Worship your body and beauty and sexual allure and you will always feel ugly. And when time and age start showing, you will die a million deaths before they finally grieve you. . . . Worship power, you will end up feeling weak and afraid, and you will need ever more power over others to numb you to your own fear. Worship your intellect, being seen as smart, you will end up feeling stupid, a fraud, always on the verge of being found out. But the insidious thing about these forms of worship is not that they're evil or sinful, it's that they're unconscious. They are default settings.

—David Foster Wallace, Commencement speech,
Kenyon College, 2005.

THE INSTINCTS OF ANIMALS ARE DIRECTED TO "NORMAL" OBJECTS OR ACtions, but very often, because of circumstances, settle on substitute objects—sometimes in unfortunate ways. Birds getting ready for births may not find the twigs they are looking for, so will use yarn, paper, scraps of wood, and other objects, if these are available, to build a nest. Pigs removed from natural soils will employ their rooting instinct on trash heaps or even on pen-mates. Ducklings removed at birth from their mothers can be "imprinted" to follow a dummy of a male mallard as if it were a mother—or even follow a human being, as the ethologist Konrad Lorenz discovered. A house cat, lacking its natural prey, will lurk and stalk other objects—for example, a toy that resembles a mouse, or even a ball of wool.

If faith is an instinct, it will require certain external or environmental prerequisites to be activated and expressed in a "normal" fashion. Coordination with an appropriate object is of the essence. In aesthetics, the maxim "Beauty is in the eye of the beholder" is true only in the sense that, without prerequisite dispositions, no aesthetic experience is possible, regardless of the quality of the object beheld. But without aesthetic objects, there would be no veridical aesthetic experience. In ethics, subject-object coordination is also necessary, though frequently overlooked.[1] For example, acting rationally is considered an important subjective moral disposition, but with the eugenics movement during the 1920s and 1930s in the United States, the sterilization of "defectives" seemed to be a "rational" solution to improving society, and in Nazi Germany even more drastic measures to purify the race were considered "rational" approaches; likewise, the assertion and defense of freedom or self-determination is thought to be an essential subjective ethical disposition, but Timothy McVeigh's bombing of the Federal Building in Oklahoma City in 1995, even if it was a sincere assertion of freedom against encroachment by the federal government, lacked obvious objective correlates. On the other hand, people may engage in actions that appear to be objectively ethical, even of the highest order, but with neutral or unethical motives—for example, the businessman who acts fairly in order to get a monopoly and drive out all other businesses; the champion of women's rights, who simply wants to endear himself to feminists to get sexual favors, or the terrorist who helps out charitable causes, in order to establish credibility before he strikes.

---

1. This coordination is discussed at length in H. Kainz, *Ethics in Context* (Washington, D.C.: Georgetown University Press, 1988), chap. 3.

PROBLEMS OF COORDINATION IN FAITH

A dysfunctional relationship between subjective and objective factors is also possible with regard to faith. It goes without saying that a Christian with a firm and intense subjective faith may express this faith through doctrines or rituals or ethical practices that are seriously deficient ways of objectifying his faith. For example, some early Christian heresies forbade marriage, Docetists thought that Jesus was just an apparition, Arians denied the divinity of Christ; some sects have justified the murder of Jews, Muslims, infidels, or heretics; some denominations have emphasized financial and social success in this world as a sign of predestination. It should also be kept in mind that, if faith is indeed paradoxically a natural instinct to *transcend* nature, as Seckler indicates,[2] the "normal" objective expression of this instinct will paradoxically include the supernatural!

It is also possible to have a faith that is objectively satisfactory, even orthodox, even encompassing the supernatural, but manifests serious subjective deficiencies, falling far short of the characteristics of faith discussed in chapter 4. A Christian painstakingly adhering to all the rules and rituals of his denomination or confession could have less subjective grounding in faith than a native or aborigine assiduously obedient to the lights of his conscience. That is, an orthodox Christian might be "into" ritual as a magical exercise and/or "into" churchgoing as a means of social acceptance and advancement; a pagan might adopt Christian rituals in the hope that they will be more conducive to wealth and success; or a successful and distinguished theologian might achieve scholarly mastery of all the Christian dogmas and laws, but with little or no personal faith.

UNSATISFACTORY OBJECTS OF FAITH

How can we understand the orientation of ancient peoples to idols? The Hebrew scriptures, for example, are full of references to attempts by leaders and prophets to draw the Israelites away from worshipping idols, to establish the worship of the true God. Were renegade Israelites in those ancient times really enraptured with statues of Baal or Moloch made of gold, bronze, wood, or other materials? Judging

2. See above, p. 101.

from the few idols that have come down to us from archaeology, we may presume that the idols were not so beautiful that aesthetic admiration was potentiated into worship. Perhaps, in some cases, worshippers thought that the idol was inhabited by some spirit, who could be entreated to bestow benefits—a successful harvest, health, progeny, or survival after death. But most likely, the real object of worship was what the particular god or goddess represented—success in love, power over others, freedom from disease or injury, good luck, or wealth.

In the sophisticated Western world of our day, idol worship in such a gross fashion is passé. Talismans and charms still exist, and some superstitious people may pray to a statue of a saint, or venerate a particular translation of the Bible, *as if* it contained something divine. But for the most part, the faith of civilized people is no longer directed toward idols, but rather toward some of the objects of natural faith discussed above.[3] One of the most popular objects is *"faith in oneself,"* extolled by people like Jesse Ventura, the former governor of Minnesota, who see religion as a "crutch for weak-minded people who need strength in numbers."[4] Self-confidence is, of course, an important psychological asset resulting from personal successes, and not incompatible with religious faith, but it can be carried to an extreme by those who for some reason have never put aside the feelings of invulnerability that oftentimes accompany adolescence. Another popular substitute faith is *faith in secular progress,* a contribution of the eighteenth-century Enlightenment, noted for the heady feeling that, by doing away with the obstacle of religious doctrines and moral injunctions, the unlimited powers of mankind for advancement would be unleashed. As the German philosopher Hegel noted, a major transformation took place in the Enlightenment, as the ideas of personal and societal perfection formerly associated with religion were transferred and relocated in secular life, so that "heaven is transplanted to earth below."[5] A scarcely less popular form of commitment is *faith in science,* on the part of cultured despisers of religion, who look to the sciences for answers to questions about the purpose of life, and of course receive only the answers that science can give—answers having to do with the development and reactions of material

---

3. See above, p. 45.
4. Interview with Jesse Ventura, *Playboy,* November 1999.
5. G. W. F. Hegel, *Phenomenology of Mind, op. cit.,* p. 598.

things, persons, and societies, insofar as they are materially observable, and quantitative measurements. Unfortunately, science can give us no precise details about the ultimate origin of matter and life, or offer us any moral norms concerning what to do with military and other technology that results from scientific progress.

In early Christianity, the heresy of Gnosticism emerged as a rival to the staid supernatural beliefs of the orthodox. The Gnostics promised heightened forms of knowledge (*Gnosis*) achieved, perhaps with Christian or pagan rituals, by a direct infusion from the divine source. In contemporary culture, New Age mysticism bears remarkable similarities to Gnosticism, emphasizing a rather amorphous attainment of "spirituality" as the counterpart of *Gnosis,* superseding all "organized religion" and the disciplines associated with it. The specific objects focused on by the New Ager initiated into spirituality can take various forms—Mother Earth, Nature, goddesses, channeling, reincarnation, Yogic or Zen forms of meditation, etc.

Satanism, either in its original form with "black masses" and black magic rituals, or in more moderate forms such as that espoused in the *Satanic Bible* of Anton LaVey (1930–97), which doesn't actually worship Satan, is partly a reaction against Christianity, but, more important an assertion of the absolute importance of oneself—something that Christians would call diabolical pride. The forms of Satanism that actually adore Satan possess a certain logical justification: Satan as a legendary supreme angel is the one to whom even the Gospel ascribes power over the whole world.[6] Satan can thus become a viable substitute for God, especially if he seems to provide the benefits and favors his adherents seek, and if these are not the sort of gifts that God would seem to be willing to grant.

PROPER OBJECTS OF RELIGIOUS FAITH

God as Object

In ancient polytheistic religions, the gods were portrayed as corporeal beings, by no means spiritual. For example, the gods of Greek and Roman religion, gods such as Zeus or Jupiter, Hermes or Mercury, Poseidon or Neptune, dwelt in an upper Olympian abode or reigned

---

6. Mt 4:9; Lk 4:6; Jn 12:31.

over "shades" of deceased personages in the netherworld regions, enjoyed sensuous delights, occasionally became involved in rivalries and battles, sometimes impregnated humans, and had very specialized mundane interests—watching over crops, wine, fertility, wars, healings, etc. As most monotheisms developed, God has been conceptualized as transcendent and incorporeal. Mormonism, in which God is portrayed as a body rather than a spirit,[7] who indeed evolved to a divine state from original human status,[8] would seem to be an exception. And Mormon claims to be monotheistic are disputed.[9]

God can be conceived either as personal or impersonal. Perhaps the best example in the modern Western world of an impersonal God is the God of deism—the God of Voltaire and Thomas Jefferson, and, more recently, the God adopted by the noted philosopher Antony Flew.[10] This is a God who has "wound up the clock" of the universe, either in a Newtonian or Einsteinian fashion, and simply lets it tick away, following the physical laws of gravity, electromagnetism, the quantum-mechanical laws of probability tabulated in wave-functions, etc. This deistic God may be deserving of respect and fear, but is obviously not the sort of God one would pray to, or hope for any providential help from, or even find attractive. In the wake of rejection of the God of Christian faith, observes Hegel, the "supreme being" of the Enlightenment turns out to be a "beyond" comparable to "the exhalation of a stale gas."[11]

What is meant by a "personal God"? This question subdivides into two distinct questions: (1) whether the God that is the object of faith is construed as a "person", and (2) whether the relationship to that God is construed as a personal relationship. For example, an ancient oriental despot would certainly be considered a person, but most or all of his subjects would hardly be considered to have a personal relationship with him. Or—a more contemporary example—the dictator Kim Jong-il of North Korea is certainly a person, but most or all of the citizens, even though they are continually urged on billboards

---

7. *Doctrine and Covenants of the Church of Jesus Christ of Latter-day Saints* (Salt Lake City, Utah; Church of Jesus Christ of Latter-Day Saints, 1982), #130:19–22; 131:7–8.

8. *Teachings of the Prophet Joseph Smith* (Salt Lake City, Deseret News Press, 1938), 345.

9. Ibid., 370. See also Fawn Brodie, *No Man Knows My History: The Life of Joseph Smith, the Mormon Prophet* (New York: Alfred Knopf, 1971), 171; and Isaiah Bennett, *Inside Mormonism: What Mormons Really Believe* (San Diego: Catholic Answers, 1999), 262 ff.

10. See above, p. 27.

11. G. W. F. Hegel, *The Phenomenology of Mind*, p. 602.

and media to "love our Great Leader," can hardly be considered to have a personal relationship with him.

What, then, is meant by a "personal relationship"? Among humans, certainly the Aristotelian concept of a "friendship of virtue" would qualify—a friendship that is limited to just a few persons and is based on mutual appreciation of one another's intrinsic goodness. The other two types of friendship that Aristotle categorizes—friendships of utility (for example, love for my handyman who is a genius at fixing things) or of pleasure (for example, love of the best sexual partner I have ever had)—would not approximate to the ideal of a personal relationship. Even acts of "charity" can be relatively personal or impersonal. Sending a check to a relief agency is commendable, but relatively impersonal; stopping to help a blind person who is having difficulty getting across the street is relatively personal—*especially* if he/she is a stranger; and one might say that the late Larry Stewart, the millionaire in Los Angeles who gave away millions to thousands of strangers in "random acts of kindness," was arguably engaged in a relatively personal way with them.

Can humans have a personal relationship with God? We are limited here to discussing God as the object of faith, and as a person, and whether or not a personal relationship between a believer and this God is possible. If a claim is made of a personal relationship, whether or not it is a real, deep, and reciprocal relationship is, of course, something in the purely private arena, and outside of our purview.

In Hinduism, Brahman as the supreme deity is a divine essence, conceived impersonally, but takes on personal forms, especially the forms of Brahma, Vishnu, and Shiva, but also of other gods. Devout Hindus claim to have had personal encounters with such gods, and the *Bhagavad Gita* is an extended narrative of such an encounter with the god Krishna. But a personal relationship with Brahman is out of the question. In Islam, Allah is absolutely transcendent, and cannot be understood at all; when he is often portrayed as "forgiving, merciful," a person seems to be implied, showing compassion to subjects, but no personal relationship is depicted. Even the prophet Muhammad himself never claims to be encountering Allah personally; all of Muhammad's prophetic operations consist of messages and commands transmitted indirectly to him by the angelic being ("Gabriel") from whom he said he received messages—with the exception of certain "Satanic verses" (verses allowing some limited polytheism in Islam), which Muhammad said were abrogated by Allah because they were inserted into the Qur'an by Satan.[12] There are a few exhortations in the Qur'an to "love Allah," but many reminders that Allah only loves those who follow the injunctions laid down through Muhammad and that Allah does not love unbelievers. One wonders what it is that Allah loves in the faithful followers, beside the fact that they are faithful and submit to the commands dictated to Muhammad. The relationship cannot be compared to the love of a father for his children, or even to the love of a creator for the works of his hands.

In the Judeo-Christian tradition, the relationship to God is construed less ambiguously as personal. The concept of God, the evolution of which is manifested in the Bible, becomes progressively more and more personal—both in the sense of God being conceptualized as a person *and* in the sense of engaging in personal relationships. In the Old Testament, Yahweh is not an abstract idea or impersonal entity, but a personal being who makes a covenant with Abraham and, for some reason, chooses a Hebrew tribe enslaved in Egypt for the implementation of this covenant, and gradually comes to depict the extension of this covenant beyond the Israelites to the world as a whole. Personal encounters take place with selected individuals. Abraham negotiates with God regarding God's contemplated punishment of Sodom,[13] God deals with Moses "face to face,"[14] and God decides to mitigate his contemplated punishment of Solomon because of the memory of his beloved, David.[15] The prophets Isaiah[16] and Jeremiah[17] used the imagery of a bride and bridegroom to describe the relationship of Israel to God—a personal relationship, with duties and reciprocities expected, but also the chance of infidelity and breakup. Many of the 150 psalms in the Bible describe an individual's longing for union with God, or thankfulness for favors, or petition for help or healing or forgiveness.

In Christianity, the relationship becomes more explicitly personal. The Son of God becomes an individual human being, refers to God as his father,[18] urges his followers to call God "father,"[19] and tells those

---

12. *The Glorious Qur'an,* trans. Mohammed Marmaduke Pickthall, (Elmhurst, N.Y.: Tahrike Tarsile Qur'an, Inc., 2000), Suras 17:73–75; 22:52–53.
13. Gn 18:26.
14. Ex 33:11.
15. 1 Kgs 11:12.
16. Is 49:18.
17. Jer 2:32.
18. Mt 26:42; Lk 2:49; Jn 8:38.
19. Mt 23:9, 6:6, 6:9; Mk 11:25; Lk 11:2.

who have followed him and shared in his labors that they are his "friends."[20] Thus in Christianity the idea of having a personal relationship with Jesus and/or the Father is not uncommon. The extremely personal quality of this relationship is exemplified in Protestants who refer to Jesus as their "personal savior" and in some Catholic saints—for example, St. Theresa of Avila, who, when complaining about sufferings and being told by Jesus, "This is the way I treat all my friends," responds familiarly, "No wonder you have so few!"

It might be objected that Christians carry the idea of personality in God *too far,* with the Trinitarian doctrine that there are three persons in one God—Father, Son, and Holy Spirit. Analogies have been made to Hinduism, in which Brahma, Vishnu, and Shiva constitute quasi-trinitarian manifestations of Brahman; and other gods give different manifestations. But Hinduism has never claimed to be a monotheistic religion. In Christianity, the oneness of God is maintained just as strongly as the Trinity of persons. The three persons in the Christian concept are not to be understood as "avatars" of the Godhead, as in Hinduism, but as absolutely identical with God. This conception is explained by some mystics as an organic relationship in which the "Godhead" expresses itself as a unity-in-diversity. There are some possible foreshadowings of this diversity in the Old Testament, in passages where Yahweh is referred to as "we."[21] At the very least the Trinitarian doctrine indicates an extreme emphasis on the *personality* of God—an emphasis unique to Christianity, and the key to interpreting what is meant by "God as object" of faith in Christianity.

The Kingdom of God as Object of Faith

The notion of a kingdom of God is distinctively a Judeo-Christian concept or "symbol." A gradual evolution of this idea is noticeable in the Old Testament, although the phrase "kingdom of God" appears only once in the Old Testament, in the Book of Wisdom[22] (included in Catholic bibles as part of the "wisdom" literature, but not considered a canonical book by Jews or Protestants). When, in the eleventh century B.C., the Israelites petitioned to have a king like many of the neighboring nations, the prophet Samuel warned them about the

---

20. Jn 15:13–15.
21. Gn 1:26, 3:22, 11:7.
22. Ws 10:9–10.

danger of monarchy, as a threat to the absolute kingship of God, the recognition of which had always been the keynote of the Hebrew confederacy.[23] After the disintegration of the Davidic monarchy, and the deportation of inhabitants of Judea to Babylon, the prophet Daniel during the exile predicts to King Nebuchadnezzar the emergence of four kingdoms, after which:

> The God of heaven will set up a kingdom that shall never be destroyed or delivered up to another people; rather, it shall break in pieces all these kingdoms and put an end to them, and it shall stand forever.[24]

After the return of a remnant to Jerusalem from the Babylonian exile in the fifth century, the idea of a Holy Commonwealth, based on the Torah as its constitution, began to crystalize.[25] The advancing concepts of the kingship of God are chronicled in the psalms of the Old Testament. For example:

> The Lord is king, robed with majesty; the Lord is robed, girded with might. . . . Your throne stands firm from of old; you are from everlasting, Lord.[26]

Some of these psalms have messianic references and are taken by Christians as foreshadowings of the coming of Christ as the Messiah —for example, in Psalm 2, Yahweh is portrayed as establishing a universal kingship:

> I myself have installed my king on Zion, my holy mountain. . . . "You are my son; today I am your father. Only ask it of me, and I will make your inheritance the nations, your possession the ends of the earth."

In the New Testament, the notion is no longer implicit or indirect. The phrase "kingdom of God," or a synonym such as "kingdom of heaven," appears over a hundred times in the Gospels. Jesus announces, "This is the time of fulfillment. The kingdom of God is at hand. Repent, and believe in the gospel."[27] The theme continues in the Acts of the Apostles[28] and throughout the Epistles. For example,

---

23. 1 Sm 10:19.
24. Dn 2:44.
25. The books of Ezra and Nehemiah describe the events leading to the reformulation.
26. Ps 93.
27. Mk 1:14–15.
28. See, for example, Acts 8:12, 19:8, 28:23, 31.

St. Paul admonishes the Romans that "the kingdom of God is not a matter of food and drink, but of righteousness, peace, and joy in the holy Spirit,"[29] and speaks to the Colossians about his "co-workers for the kingdom of God."[30]

Both Protestant and Catholic theologians and Scripture scholars converge in holding that the symbol of the kingdom of God is the primary message of the Gospel.[31] Disputes remain, however, as to whether in Christianity the Kingdom is conceived as something present here and now ("realized eschatology") or an apocalyptic event consistently to be understood of the future ("consistent eschatology").[32] Most contemporary exegetes lean toward the interpretation of a present Kingdom of God; but the important and ongoing debate among Christians down through the centuries has been regarding the question whether this present kingdom is the *Church* or not, and, if it is the Church, whether it should be construed as a visible church or an invisible church.[33]

Regardless of which interpretation is adopted, it is of crucial importance, for the future of Christianity and civilization, that the Kingdom of God *not* be conceived as a temporal kingdom, needing to be established in this world. As Aldous Huxley notes, any ideology that considers it imperative to establish an envisioned order in this world and in time will inevitably lead to utilization of "unlimited violence to achieve their ends."[34] With regard to religion, we may agree with Huxley that:

> The reign of violence will never come to an end until . . . there is a worldwide rejection of all the political pseudo-religions, which place man's supreme good in future time and therefore justify and commend the commission of every sort of present iniquity as a means to that end.[35]

In the history of Christianity, excesses such as the Inquisition and witch burnings—for which there is no justification in the New Testament—are explainable as results of an overemphasis on establishing

---

29. Rom 14:17–18.
30. Col 4:11.
31. See H. Kainz, "New Testament Conceptualization of Messianic Fulfillment," in *Democracy and the "Kingdom of God"* (Dordrecht: Kluwer, 1993) chap. 6.
32. See ibid., chap. 9, "The Dialectics of Christian Interpretation."
33. Ibid., chap. 13, "How Visible can a 'City of God' be?"
34. Aldous Huxley, *The Perennial Philosophy* (New York: Harper Colophon Books, 1945), 193.
35. Ibid., 200.

the Kingdom of God now *on earth*—in spite of Jesus's admonition that his kingdom is "not of this world";[36] and as results of the fusion of Church and state by Protestants or Catholics who confused the interests of God and Caesar, contrary to the Gospel admonitions.[37] But those who point to the Crusades as an example of aggression entailed by Christianity almost always fail to take into account the fact that there would have been no Crusade if the Muslims hadn't invaded and captured Jerusalem in A.D. 638, and then Syria, Egypt, and many Christian countries.

An Islamic counterpart of the Christian belief in the Kingdom of God is Mahdism—the belief that the final victory of Islam over the whole world will be overseen by a messianic figure, the Mahdi, who will establish the final world Caliphate enforcing Sharia law. Various versions of Mahdism are subscribed to by both Shiite and Sunni Muslims.[38] Going beyond the Christian goal of preaching the Gospel throughout the world to save all humans, Islamic eschatology enjoins Muslims to fight against unbelievers until they either are converted, or conquered, or agree to accept a subordinate position requiring payment of taxes and no public displays of non-Muslim beliefs:

> Slay the idolaters wherever ye find them, and take them (captive), and besiege them, and prepare for them each ambush. But if they repent and establish worship and pay the poor-due, then leave their way free. . . . Fight against such of those who have been given the Scripture [Christians and Jews] as believe not in Allah nor the Last Day, and [who] forbid not that which Allah hath forbidden by His messenger [Muhammad], and follow not the religion of truth, until they pay the tribute readily, being brought low.[39]

Recent remarks have been made by Iranian President Mahmoud Ahmadinejad to the effect that he expects the imminent coming of al-Mahdi. In conjunction with the nuclear ambitions of Ahmadinejad, and his stated goal of annihilating the state of Israel, the world has received a clear contemporary ominous example of the danger of merging "Caesar" and God in the pursuit of the expansion of any religiously inspired "kingdom."

36. Jn 8:23; 18:36.
37. Mt 22:21; Mk 12:17; Lk 20:25.
38. See Mary Habeck, *Knowing the Enemy: Jihadist Ideology and the War on Terror* (New Haven, Conn.: Yale University Press, 2006).

Eternal Life as an Object of Faith

Theories concerning the immortality of the human soul have been a constant in the history of Western philosophy, even before the advent of Christianity. Plato, for instance, in his dialogue, *Phaedo,* comes to the conclusion that our ideas of perfection, such as "equality" and "goodness," are beyond the parameters of the changing material world, and thus indicate that the soul that harbors them must be immune to the disintegration to which material beings are subject;[40] Plato also theorized that the soul that contemplates the divine must have divine and immortal qualities itself.[41] Plato's disciple, Aristotle, similarly concludes from the human power of forming universal concepts that there must be some element of the human soul that does not die.[42]

In our day, in which the givens of empirical science are very often the first source to be consulted, the widespread phenomenon of Near Death Experiences (NDEs), due to contemporary medical advances in resuscitation technology, offers numerous case studies of people who reported being in an intensively conscious state even after being pronounced "clinically dead."[43] NDE reports about experiences of entering into another dimension, as well as philosophical speculation, can present us with a strong probability of an "afterlife"—but only a probability. We are looking for something a bit more conclusive. In a "best-case scenario," the most conclusive evidence would be a "word of God," as Plato himself indirectly suggested:

> [One who seeks the truth about immortality] should persevere until he has achieved one of these things: either he should discover, or be taught the truth about them; or, if this be impossible, I would have him take the best and most irrefragable of human theories, and let this be the raft upon which he sails through life—not without risk, as I admit, if he cannot find some word of God which will more surely and safely carry him.[44]

Without any revelation from God, we can discern a possibility, maybe even a strong probability, of a continuance of human life after death.

39. Sura 9:5, 29.
40. Plato, *Phaedo,* 75c–75d, 79d.
41. Ibid., 84a–84c.
42. Aristotle, *De anima* III, 5.
43. For an analysis of such cases and traditional philosophical arguments, see H. Kainz, *The Philosophy of Human Nature* (Chicago: Open Court, 2007), chap. 12.
44. Plato, *Phaedo,* 85b–85e.

But for Christians (and also for Jews, if Professors Blumenthal and Levenson are correct)[45] the "word of God" that Plato was hoping for has actually been spoken and promulgated. The promise of "eternal life" certainly pervades all of the New Testament.[46] And this promise is not just an abstract possibility, such as that suggested by philosophers and others. Rather, it is "possibility" in the sense of a psychic potential or power—analogous to the potential of a gifted person for accomplishing certain things beyond the reach of others, or the proven ability of an athlete to match or break a certain record. This potential, in the Christian construal, is not something superadded to the human soul at the time of death, but begins here and now, as the experience of eternal life—often veiled, but on occasion impinging with some force on one's sensibility.

According to the Christian Gospel, all humans who die will be resurrected,[47] and in heaven "the righteous will shine like the sun in the kingdom of their Father"[48] and have the ability to "see God,"[49] and "neither marry nor are given in marriage but are like the angels in heaven."[50] The model for what St. Paul calls the resurrected "spiritual body" is the body of Jesus after his resurrection, which demonstrated power over matter (being able to go through walls,[51] appear and disappear suddenly,[52] and ascend from the earth),[53] but also possessed the quite material ability to cook for his disciples and eat,[54] and be touched by his disciples.[55]

This view of heaven, as a state in which people who die in God's grace will have glorified bodies, and go beyond faith to actually see God, is the most sublime concept of immortality in any religion, and is held by most Christians. Sharp contrasts and contradictions to this concept are found in non-Christian religions, such as Hinduism, with its emphasis on multiple reincarnations, and Islam, which, although

---

45. See above, p. 78.
46. See, for example, Lk 10:25; Jn 6:69, 17:2–3; Acts 13:46; Rom 2:7; 1 Tm 6:12; 1 Jn 3:15, 5:11–13.
47. Mk 12:25; Lk 14:14, 20:35–36; Jn 5:29, 11:24–25.
48. Mt 13:43.
49. Mt 5:8.
50. Mt 22:30
51. Jn 20:19.
52. Mk 16:12, 14; Lk 24:31, 24:36.
53. Mk 16:19; Lk 24:51.
54. Lk 24:42; Jn 21:13.
55. Lk 24:39; Jn 20:17, 20:27.

it includes no clear doctrine of bodily resurrection, depicts heaven as "gardens beneath which rivers flow,"[56] whose inhabitants will wear fine clothing and gold bracelets, recline on couches, be served with delicious drinks, and in general, be regaled with all manner of sensuous delights:

> (Ye) who believed Our revelations and were self-surrendered, enter the Garden, ye and your wives, to be made glad. Therein are brought round for them trays of gold and goblets, and therein is all that souls desire and eyes find sweet. And ye are immortal therein. This is the Garden which ye are made to inherit because of what ye used to do. Therein for you is fruit in plenty whence to eat.[57]

The peak pleasures of heaven for virtuous male Muslims consist of the constant attentions of beautiful girls, *houris:* "Lo! Those who kept their duty will be in a place secure, amid gardens and water-springs, attired in silk and silk embroidery, facing one another. Even so (it will be). And We [Allah] shall wed them unto fair ones with wide, lovely eyes."[58] Handsome boys will also help to fulfill all their desires.[59]

Along with Muslims, who include conjugal bliss among the sensuous delights of heaven, Mormons, many of whom claim to be Christian, consider "celestial marriage" as an indispensable aspect of heaven, in spite of Jesus's clear admonition to the Sadducees that resurrected persons "neither marry nor are given in marriage." Mormons believe they will optimally arrive at the status of "gods and goddesses" in the next life through marriage and the "sealing" of children to themselves in this life, preferably in the Mormon Temple.

It goes without saying that living like an angel and seeing God face to face may not seem like an attractive goal to many people—even many Christians will try to reinterpret eternal life as something more conformable to our concepts of an enjoyable secular life. In particular, the Christian concept seems to be missing the aspect of social relatedness, which seems indispensable for happiness in this life, and which is emphasized almost exclusively in concepts of the afterlife in non-Christian religions. St. Thomas Aquinas considers this question in his *Summa:*

---

56. See, for example, Qur'an 2:25, 4:57, 18.31, 22:23, 47:15.
57. Qur'an 43:69–73.
58. Qur'an 44:51–54.; see also 52:20, 55:56, 78:31.
59. Qur'an 52:54; 56:17.

If we speak about the perfect happiness that will be attained in the next life, the society of friends is not a matter of necessity for happiness in that state. For a person possesses the complete fulfillment of his/her perfection in God. But the society of friends does contribute to the enhancement of that happiness.[60]

Aquinas then goes on to make a distinction between intrinsic and extrinsic aspects of happiness. If a soul is united with God and attains the beatific vision, his or her internal experience of happiness will be so complete that nothing more could be required for it. In the present life, we have a need for friends in order to have complete happiness, but this will not be the case in the next life. But externally, the reflection of this complete happiness among souls will provide an external enhancement. Aquinas quotes Augustine:

> "Extrinsically, if we can speak about an enhancement of this blessed state, possibly this can only happen insofar as the blessed see one another and rejoice in God for this association."[61]

The Christian concept of the beatific vision is a challenge to the imagination. We have to visualize a state of complete bliss that fulfills every need without exception, but includes the possibility of spontaneously sharing the reflections of that bliss with others—perhaps analogously to the way that God, with no need to create, spontaneously has shared His goodness with Creatures.

60. *S.T.* I-II q. 4, a. 8.
61. Ibid.

7

The Wider Orbit of Faith in the World

[In my book, *On the True Religion,*] my statement, "in our times the most secure and certain salvation is through knowing and following the Christian religion," concerned the name, not the reality behind the name. For what is now called the Christian religion existed even among the ancients and was not lacking from the beginning of the human race until Christ came in the flesh, from which time the true, presently existing religion, began to be called "Christian."

—Augustine, The Retractions I, 13, 3.

God's directions and revelations were indeed entrusted to this nation [the Jews] but were not intended for it alone; in their further unfolding they are to embrace all nations and in their fuller light to establish one great community of all peoples and all nations under the rule of God.

—Johann Sebastian Drey,
Brief Introduction to the Study of Theology, §27

Those also can attain to salvation who through no fault of their own do not know the Gospel of Christ or His Church, yet sincerely seek God and moved by grace strive by their deeds to do His will as it is known to them through the dictates of conscience.

—Pope Paul VI, Lumen Gentium

Then Peter proceeded to speak and said, "In truth, I see that God shows no partiality. Rather, in every nation whoever fears him and acts uprightly is acceptable to him."

—Acts 10:34

THE PROBLEM OF SALVATION FOR ALL

IN THE OLD TESTAMENT, THERE ARE SOME INDICATIONS THAT THE MEANS of salvation entrusted by Yahweh through Moses to the Israelites are meant to be extended to all nations;[1] but in the New Testament, the message that God wishes eternal salvation for all people becomes loud and clear.[2] Indeed, the tradition of both the Old and the New Testaments considers numerous "pagans" to be among the saved— Abel, whose sacrifices were acceptable to God;[3] Enoch the Babylonian, who was taken up bodily into heaven[4] and is recognized in the Roman Catholic martyrology as a pagan saint; Abraham's brother, Lot, ancestor of the Moabites, who did not participate in the Abrahamic covenant, and who is also listed as a saint in the Roman martyrology; the Babylonian, Noah (with whom God made a covenant, "sealed" with a rainbow); Job from Idumea; Melchisidech, King of Salem before it became Jerusalem; and the Arabian Queen of Saba (now Yemen). God's covenant with Abraham, signified by ritual circumcision, also predated the Mosaic covenant and the Torah.[5] For theologians, this raises the question concerning the means of salvation outside of the ambit of both the Mosaic Law and the Law of Grace. A common response among Catholic theologians is that the tenets of natural law have always been available to rational creatures, and that those who existed in the earliest eras of salvation history were saved by following the natural law, spelled out in some detail by God to Noah after the Great Flood:

> For your own lifeblood . . . I will demand an accounting: from every animal I will demand it, and from man in regard to his fellow man I will demand an accounting for human life. If anyone sheds the blood of man, by man shall his blood be shed: For in the image of God has man been made. Be fertile, then, and multiply; abound on earth and subdue it.[6]

Thus Aquinas, in response to the question of whether those who existed in the natural-law condition were saved by implementing the pre-

---

1. Is 2:2–4, 42:6, 45:22–24, 51:4–5.
2. Mt 21:31; Jn 1:7, 5:23; Rom 5:18; Eph 3:9; 1 Tm 2:1, 2:4, 4:10.
3. Gn 4:4.
4. Gn 5:24.
5. In the Old and New Testaments, a gradual progression of covenants with God is discernible. The covenant with Noah promised no further destruction of the world by flooding; the covenant with Abraham promised land and progeny; the covenant with Moses promised special protection for Israelites, as long as they adhered to the laws of the Pentateuch; the covenant with David promised a kingship that would last eternally; and the new covenant or New Testament of Christianity established Christ as the eternal king promised in the Davidic line, and was sealed in Christ's blood.
6. Gn 9:5–7.

scriptions of the natural law, offers the following clarification: "Although nature per se could not suffice for the knowledge of a Redeemer, nevertheless it did suffice along with the written law at the time of the [Mosaic] law; and, before the law, it sufficed with assistance from grace."[7] By means of this "assistance of grace," those who "knew nothing about the law of Moses" were saved "through an implicit faith in a redeemer, indeterminately implying this faith through their knowledge of God, or through their knowledge of those taught by God, whoever these latter might be."[8] (Aquinas includes among "those taught by God" two then-legendary personages: a pre-Christian Sybil whose prophecy, concerning judgment by a future "king of heaven," is recounted in Virgil's *Eclogues;* and someone whose body was found during the reign of Constantine, allegedly containing a golden plate with a pre-Christian inscription about his or her belief in the coming of Christ.)

But what about those who have lived *after* the coming of Christ and the spread of the Christian Gospel? As Seckler observes, it seems logical to extend the same sort of reasoning to all those who after the advent of Christ, because of conditions beyond their control, have been outside the pale of God's salvific interventions in human history:

> It seems intrinsically legitimate to extend that providential faith that was looked upon as sufficient for the pagans before the Gospel, also to those after the Christian era who were not evangelized. For the situation of salvation history which was changed through the Incarnation and the New Testament Kerygma relates to new conditions, but a presupposition for access to these conditions by the believing individual seems to be that he be made acquainted with these conditions.[9]

This presents a theological problem, however, insofar as Christian tradition, subscribed to by Catholics, Orthodox, and Protestants in various degrees, maintains, on the one hand, that Christ willed all persons to be saved, but, on the other hand, that salvation now, in the "age of grace," requires baptism and/or explicit faith in Christ as savior. This posed a problem for scholastic theologians in Aquinas's time

---

7. *In IV libros Sententiarum Commentaria, ex manuscriptis bibliothecae Tolosanae conuentus Sancti Thomae Aquinatis.* Tolosae, Apus Colomerium, 1649–52. (Ridgewood, N.J.: Gregg Press, 1964), vol. 3, d. 25, q. 2, a 2, quaestiuncula 2, arg 4 and ad 4. (This work will hereafter be abbreviated as *In Sent.*)

8. Ibid., ad 3.

also, and the solution he came up with, in his early works, was a solution commonly presented by his contemporaries:

> For a man seeking salvation, God is not and has never been absent.[10] It pertains to divine providence that God provide for each person what is necessary for salvation, as long as there is no impediment on the part of the individual. For if someone brought up in the wilderness follows the lead of natural reason in desiring the good and fleeing evil, *it is to be held with certainty* that God will reveal to him whatever is necessary to be believed.[11]

In other words, God will provide all that is necessary for all to be saved, even if they have never had access to evangelization. The example that Aquinas gives, of an aborigine in the wilderness, was considered to be an extreme case. In such an extreme case, Aquinas states with great confidence that God will either send a preacher or bring about a private enlightenment.[12]

Aquinas also proposes a similar solution for someone who lives in the midst of unbelievers and is prevented from hearing anything about the faith:

> If such a person does whatever is in his power to seek salvation, God will provide salvific means to him in the manner just indicated [that is, by sending a preacher or by a special revelation].[13]

With regard to this solution, Seckler observes:

> With this [idea of the alternative illumination of pagans who did not have the benefit of evangelization] Thomas' question about the salvation of the non-evangelized seems to be addressed, and not a few authors see in this answer—that God will in any case send a preacher or effect a private enlightenment—a definite solution, at least for the question raised by Aquinas.[14]

---

9. Seckler, 237.

10. *In Sent.*, vol. 3, d 25, q 2, a 1, sol 1, ad 1.

11. *De Veritate* 14, 11, ad 1. Italics added.

12. *In Sent.*, vol. 2, d 28, q 1, a 4, ad 4; vol. 3, d 25, q 1, solutio 1, ad 1, et ad 2; a 2, solutio 2c. See also *Opera omnia*, Leonine edition (Rome, 1972) tome 22, vol. 2, *Quaestiones disputatae de veritate*, q 14, a 11, ad 1.

13. *In Sent.*, vol. 3, d 25, q. 2, a.1. quaestiuncula 1, ad 2. Aquinas responds to this challenge similarly in *De veritate* 14, II, ad 1.

14. Seckler, 239.

However, this sanguine response to the question of the salvation of the "non-evangelized" is exclusively a characteristic of Aquinas's early works. In his later works, especially the *Summa,* which was left unfinished because of his death, he seemed to be following Augustine in a stricter interpretation of "no salvation outside the Church." Seckler comments that Aquinas was living at a time when it was presumed that the Gospel had been effectively spread throughout the world, so that the example of "someone living in the wild" seemed to be speculative and unrealistic—although medievals then were receiving occasional faint intimations of unexplored territories and unknown peoples.[15] Thus in the *Summa* he allows for a possible prophetic and salvific foreshadowing of the coming of a messiah in the pagan world prior to Christianity,[16] but refrains from speculating about the salvation of the non-evangelized after the advent of Christianity.

But Aquinas's silence in his later works regarding this question was not absolute. Seckler points out[17] that, in the *Summa,* in his treatment of the baptism of the "pagan" centurion Cornelius by St. Peter, Aquinas provides a solution that is nothing less than astonishing, and also seems to bring us back to the fundamental question of a faith-instinct. Aquinas says:

> *Cornelius was not an unbeliever.* Otherwise his actions would not have been acceptable to God, whom no one is able to please without faith. But Cornelius had an implicit faith, *at a time when the Gospel was not yet manifested.* Thus Peter was sent to him in order to instruct him fully in the faith.[18]

The various above-mentioned statements by Aquinas about the possibility of implicit faith in a *future* redeemer were relevant to the pre-Christian era. But after the coming of Christ, while the Gospel was just beginning to be spread, according to the text just mentioned, an implicit faith in the Redeemer who has already come is also presupposed. Aquinas's mention here of "implicit faith" seems reminiscent of Tertullian's *anima naturaliter Christiana,* and points forward to Karl Rahner's depiction of the "anonymous Christian," as "the pagan after the beginning of the Christian mission, who lives in the state of Christ's grace through faith, hope and love, yet who has no explicit

---

15. Ibid., 239–40.
16. *S. T.* II-II, 2, 7, ad 3.
17. Seckler, 242.
18. *S. T.* II-II, 10, 4, ad 3. Italics added.

knowledge of the fact that his life is orientated in grace-given salvation to Jesus Christ."[19] Aquinas is referring to the time when "the Gospel was not yet manifested," while Rahner refers to the time "after the beginning of the Christian mission." If Seckler is correct that Aquinas, in view of the medieval geographical knowledge, mistakenly thought that the Gospel had indeed "been manifested," they are both referring to the same post-Christianity realm of the "non-evangelized."

THE SALVATION OF THE NON-EVANGELIZED: SECKLER'S SOLUTION

What is the minimum requisite "content" for faith? Seckler, following Aquinas's commentary on Hebrews 11:6, places the minimum at two essentials: (1) belief in the existence of God, and (2) further belief that this God governs the world providently.[20] The formal, conceptual knowledge of God as the ultimate lawgiver, as a result of reflection, is not necessarily required, but only the "existential" knowledge that nature, as the voice of God, gives us through our instinctive awakening to obligation as we arrive at the age of reason. Conscience itself is our initial encounter with the voice of God.[21]

This initial encounter, however, is not reducible to a moral prompting to do this or that specific deed, but something more fundamental and significant: the impetus to implement the good and the true *just because it is good and true.*[22] The existential state that Seckler is referring to here is reminiscent of what Kierkegaard called "the choice of oneself": the fundamental choice that puts an individual for the first time on the ethical level of existence.[23] But Seckler goes further: this initial awakening to "the ethical" amounts to a transcendence of the sphere of immanent secular utilities and facilitates the dawning of religious awareness.[24]

19. *Theological Investigations,* vol. 14, Trans. David Bourke (London: Darton, Longman & Todd), 283.

20. Seckler, p. 236. Cf. Aquinas's commentary, *In Hebraeos* ll, 2: "For someone to come to God, it is necessary to believe that he exists, i.e., because of God's eternity (see Exodus II, 14: 'He who exists has sent me.') Secondly, it is necessary to know that God provides for things. Otherwise, no one would draw nigh to Him, unless he hoped for some remuneration. For a wage is what a man seeks in his labor. . . . And the wage in this case is nothing other than God Himself."

21. Seckler, 254.

22. Ibid., 250.

23. Søren Kierkegaard, *Either/Or,* trans. Walter Lowrie (New York: Anchor, 1959), II, 327.

24. Seckler, 250.

Since the voice of nature—heart, conscience, spirit—is the voice of God, who manifests Himself in nature as salvific power; and since all that is true, whoever propounds it, is from the Holy Spirit—: For this reason the obedience in reference to the voice of nature is not just formal fulfillment of duty, but personal response with regard to salvation, and the redemption of fundamental human value—but always with the proviso that this knowledge, implicit in the first moral act of a man situated in the emergence of ethical consciousness, is not construed conceptually, although it is still true.[25]

What seems to be naturally good impulses, leading an individual to listen to conscience and the promptings of the heart, and expressions of sympathy and empathy, is not just the voice of nature, but the voice of God.[26] And this development *ipso facto* constitutes the necessary preparation for grace, and can result in justification:

One who is prepared for grace, who acts according to his conscience, is justified insofar as he is concerned for his salvation and realizes the good and the true according to his abilities. He does not even have to wait for a preacher or for a private revelation, in order that his good will and his readiness for faith might be realized; rather, *insofar* as he acts according to conscience, grace comes to him.[27]

THE FAITH-INSTINCT AS A *POTENTIA OBEDIENTIALIS*

In the philosophical theology of Thomas Aquinas, and medieval scholasticism in general, significant effort and multiple discussions were devoted to the differentiation and specific properties of the various "potencies" associated with human nature. Among these potencies was a rather unique potency called the "obediential potency" (*potentia obedientialis*), which Aquinas defines in one place as follows:

In the human soul there is a potency which is passive in relationship to [God], who is able to elevate any creature to a state of higher actuality, to which it could not be elevated through any natural agent; and this potency is commonly referred to as the "obediential potency" in creatures.[28]

---

25. Ibid., p. 257.
26. Ibid., 252, 264.
27. Ibid., 251.
28. *S.T.* III, q. 11, a. 1c. See also q. 1, a.3, ad 3. In *"Active and Passive Potency" in Thomistic Angelology* (The Hague: Nijoff, 1972), I include an extensive analysis of the various potencies distinguished by Aquinas, including the obediential potency.

This is an extremely paradoxical capacity, a concomitant to what Henri de Lubac refers to as the paradoxical capacity of pure nature (*natura pura*) to be affected and transformed by grace.[29] The faith-instinct, as a natural potency for the supernatural, ostensibly falls into the same category, but, as with any obediential potency, poses metaphysical questions. Is human nature embedded with the capacity to be raised to the supernatural, even to see God, from the outset? Or does the advent of grace create a capacity that was not there originally? Max Seckler sees two disparate responses to this problematic in the theological approaches of Karl Rahner and Henri de Lubac. According to Seckler, Rahner held to a *natura pura* that never quite came into contact with grace, although it had an aptitude for elevation by grace, while de Lubac saw grace and faith not as some miraculous superadded emolument, but as implicit within the *desiderium naturale*, the natural desire of humans for happiness.[30] Seckler maintains that de Lubac offers an approach closer to the Thomistic connotation of the obediential potency.

If indeed every human being is endowed with this natural orientation to faith, we may, at this juncture, according to Seckler, go beyond Aquinas to suggest some ecumenical implications, which seem to be logically entailed by our supposition that every human has an "implicit faith." This supposition gives us the basis and the incentive for reexamining the question about the salvation of those outside the parameters of the Gospel:

> Of special importance is the concept of *fides implicita* and the "non-Thomistic" transition from the conceptual to the vital and existential implication of the Faith-object in the elementary and embryonic act of faith. Thus a decision is already made in the first moral act of each man concerning salvation and its opposite—an insight that is grounded in the last analysis in the thesis about the convertibility of the ethical-good with the religious-good. Whoever orients his life toward ultimate values does this by means of the meaning of human nature, not without the grace that is directly at work here under the concealed form of the religious instinct.[31]

---

29. Henri de Lubac, "The Paradox Overcome in Faith," chap. 9 in *The Mystery of the Supernatural* (New York: Herder & Herder, 1967).

30. Max Seckler, "Potentia oboedientialis bei Karl Rahner (1904–84) und Henri de Lubac (1896–1991)," *Gregorianum* 78, no. 4, (1997) 699–718.

31. Seckler, 267.

Seckler concludes "non-Thomistically" as follows: (1) The *initial* decisions for faith will probably consist, not in what we might call explicit faith-commitments, e.g., assent to certain doctrines, but rather in the "first moral act," the act which has to do with the dawning of an understanding of the ultimate meaning of life and our response to that understanding; (2) the convertibility of the ethical-good with the religious-good *seems* to imply that a commitment to ultimate values, e.g., the natural law, may be a manifestation of faith, even without any of the explicit commitments that we usually associate with faith; and 3) "preaching the faith," e.g., the Christian faith, would be understood not as implanting an understanding and commitment that was not previously present, but rather as supporting, building upon, redirecting, correcting and/or shepherding a faith that was already there.

The "will to believe," as Seckler construes it, like the *desiderium naturale* of de Lubac, does not need to lie in wait for an external influx of grace, but unfolds teleologically to implement a natural orientation:

> The will to believe is not a decision brought about by actual grace, or an intellectual deposit regarded "as true," but the ethical expression, concretized in a message, of an ontic law—a law that lies in the nature of things and coordinates them from within.[32]

But the ultimate goal of this natural drive is not natural, but *supernatural*. Thus someone who arrives by the use of natural reason at a theistic or deistic *conceptual* belief in the existence of a Supreme Being has taken only an intermediate, and not necessarily significant, step toward this goal:

> In terms of basic materials, God's existence and providence could be deduced from evidence in created things. A man *in a purely natural condition* could, on the basis of such evidence, attain to a firm natural knowledge about God, the truth of which would be demonstrated through the natural light of reason, but which would not in any way transcend the order of nature. But the very same material contents of knowledge could for this or that concrete existing man become a calling to salvific knowledge, since its objective expression actually leads to the God of revelation, who as the God of salvation (and not as the God of a hypothetical *pure nature*)

32. Ibid.

operates in all things, and whose plan of salvation is maintained in the conception of Providence.[33]

ALTERNATIVE OR SUBSTITUTE "MATERIALS" FOR FAITH

Discussion of the faith-instinct, of course, emphasizes the *subjective* basis for faith. As Seckler observes, it is the indispensible prerequisite that allows "hearing" to take place, with openness to revelation, and prepares the soul to seek out and follow along the path of salvation.[34] But what if, as Aquinas seems to insist in the above-mentioned passages, *some* external material—the aspect of faith that is "heard"—is requisite for the full activation of faith, in addition to the awakening of conscience through the faith-instinct? In lieu of the miracle of inspiration that Aquinas referred to as a possibility, or the providential sending of a preacher to apparently unreachable places, would not some objective instigations be requisite to activate a properly disposed faith-instinct? Various possibilities suggest themselves, observes Seckler, if we consider the environment and culture and traditions that are relevant to many who have never encountered the revelation of the Gospel explicitly:

> If natural knowledge does not suffice as a salvific act, and if one still does not want to give up on the real possibility of salvation, the unavoidable question is raised about the mediation of the materials of faith necessitated for salvation. In principle there are a number of possibilities that offer a basis for the mediation of these materials: namely, the still-transmitted fragments of a primal revelation once promulgated to men; the echo of the Decalogue in the ethical codes of almost all peoples; the penetrating atmosphere in pagan milieux, recognized or unrecognized, of Christian revelation as it was expressed in the public opinions and rumors of medievals; and finally, silent preaching through the life of holy persons.[35]

Seckler's suggestions seem to be most relevant to Western civilization, which has been heavily influenced by the Judeo-Christian tradition and its ethical codes; to the contemporary European countries,

33. Ibid., 246.
34. Ibid., 264.
35. Ibid., 244.

well-supplied with architectural and artistic and literary reminders of past Christian culture, although lacking in the number of dedicated Christians present in yesteryears; and/or to the occasional exemplary Christian, whose everyday life is testimony to the Gospel and a "sermon in itself." But there are much more difficult cases to be considered—perhaps the contemporary counterpart to the scenarios of the "aborigines in the forest" that Aquinas cited in the texts mentioned above.

CHRISTIANITY AND THE RELATION TO THE "OUTER PERIMETERS" OF FAITH

A recent book[36] narrates a story of the sort of miraculous interventions that Aquinas in his early works may have had in mind. The subject of the book, Liu Zhenying, later called "Brother Yun," lived in a farming village in China's Henan province. During Chairman Mao's "Cultural Revolution" in 1974, when his father was on the brink of death from lung cancer, his mother received an internal spiritual "locution" bringing back distant memories of Christianity and the Bibles that had been confiscated throughout China in previous years. She and her family started praying incessantly to Jesus, and Yun's father was completely cured. Yun, age sixteen, then began praying for a Bible so that he could find out more about this "Jesus." To possess a Bible was a crime punishable by prison, torture, and even death; but eventually a Bible was brought to him after an underground evangelist in a neighboring village had received a vision telling him that Yun needed the Bible that had been buried in a can deep in the ground. Yun went to work, memorizing verbatim the various chapters of the Bible, and began spreading his knowledge wherever and whenever possible. Numerous healings and exorcisms began to take place, visions, miraculous appearances, miraculous multiplication of food. Yun was imprisoned three times for a total of seven years, undergoing incredible torture and engaging in a fast from all food and drink for seventy-four days. Miraculous escapes from prison reminiscent of incidents in the Acts of the Apostles took place. As a wanted "criminal," he was finally able to escape to freedom in Germany, after help-

36. Brother Yun and Paul Hattaway, *The Heavenly Man* (Grand Rapids, Mich.: Monarch Books, 2002).

ing to lay the groundwork for a network of "house churches" spreading throughout China and comprising millions of "underground" Christians.

In lieu of such miraculous interventions, it is easy to imagine numerous situations in which there would be little or no external "materials" offering inducement to supernatural faith. Such situations offer significant "test cases"—if indeed the faith-instinct is paradoxically oriented to the supernatural, and if indeed something objective corresponding to the subjective disposition toward faith is required.

Some significant obstacles to the "hearing" of the message of the Christian faith are posed by the major "natural" religions—religions/philosophies that emerged prior to Christianity and even to Judaism, in the Eastern world. Buddhism has always posed major impediments, because of its complete lack of belief in a deity or immortality in the Christian sense, as well as epistemological differences regarding the reality of the material world. In China, Taoism and popular religion are at least open to the notion of a transcendent deity, and Confucianism finds considerable resonance in the ethics of many Christian cultures; Matteo Ricci and other Christian missionaries in past centuries have capitalized on an openness to the Christian faith, at present still hindered by political restrictions in the Peoples Republic. Hinduism, with a clear belief in a supreme deity, and the concomitant belief in the trinity of Brahma-Vishnu-Shiva, as well as a highly developed Yogic mystical tradition, offers the least problematic environment for the message of the Christian faith; and Christian missionaries, such as Father Bede Griffiths, who died in 1993 in a thatched hut at Shantivanam in South India, have offered evidence of the remarkable assimilability of Christianity and Hinduism. But obstacles to acceptance of the Christian faith in India are still formidable, because of polytheistic elements, belief in reincarnation, and rituals still embedded in culture, such as the caste system and the ritual suicide of widows.

But the cases in our day *most* similar to, and even *more* formidable than, Aquinas' scenario of "an aborigine in the forest" are situations in which *ideologies* present an almost impermeable blockage to hearing anything about the Christian faith. In North Korea, in spite of constitutional assurances of the freedom of religion (along with "freedom to *oppose* religion"), the official state religion cultivates devotion to the deceased "Great Leader" Kim Il-sung and today's "Dear Leader," his son Kim Jong-il. Aside from a few churches permitted by the state, especially for foreign visitors, any public practicing or preaching of the Christian faith is prohibited and subject to severe punishment.

An even more severe and almost insuperable obstacle to Christian faith is Islamic ideology, widespread and incorporated constitutionally in numerous Middle Eastern states. Although the early segments of the Muslim scripture, the Qur'an, refer to accommodation and mutual tolerance of Muslims for Christians and Jews, the later segments of the Qur'an, dictated by Muhammad after his flight from Mecca to Medina, where he became a powerful warlord, rule out any association with Christians as equals. Thus Sura 5:51 of the Qur'an admonishes all Muslims: "O ye who believe! Take not Jews and Christians for friends. He among you who would take them for friends is (one) of them. Lo! Allah guideth not wrongdoing folk." And Sura 9 at great length mandates persecution of Christians until they either convert or are vanquished, or surrender and become subject to Muslim leadership, with payment of special taxes. Wherever ideological Islam prevails, the building of churches and any public manifestation of Christian rituals are disallowed, Bibles and crosses cannot be sold or displayed. The laws of Saudi Arabia, Iran, Sudan, Yemen, Mauritania, and Afghanistan mandate the death penalty for any Muslim who converts to another religion (the implementation of these laws has sometimes been mitigated, due to opposition from the international community). In short, the impossibility of contact with the Christian faith by a Muslim citizen in such closed societies is comparable to, or even greater than, the impossibility experienced by Aquinas's hypothetical "aborigine."

In such cases, presuming that no miraculous divine interventions, such as those that Aquinas speculated about, take place, and presuming that elements of Christianity reflected in culture, literature, architecture, etc., are nonexistent, Seckler, following Aquinas, directs us to focus on what seems to be the bare minimum for salvation— namely, that an individual does *"das Seine,"* which is meant to be the German equivalent of what Aquinas referred to as *"faciens quod in se est"*[37]—expressions that might be translated in English as "following one's conscience" or "following the laws of one's nature:"

> For a person who has not been evangelized, the life pattern that is unavoidably necessary, but also sufficient for faith, justification and salvation

37. *In Sent.* III, d. 25, q. 2, a. 1, quaestiuncula 1, ad 2.

consists in the fact that, insofar as he acts according to conscience, he is following his inner instinct and, in his concern for his salvation through fidelity, humility and obedience, he abandons his autonomous human behavior.[38]

In the framework of Aquinas's teaching, this indispensable fidelity would amount to adherence to the primary natural laws: respect for life, fulfillment of family obligations, search for the truth, and contribution to harmonious societal structures.[39]

FAITH AND FALSE PROPHETS

Any instinct, as was mentioned above,[40] requires certain external prerequisites in order to be activated and function normally. Without the proper objects, it can be diverted onto substitute objects. By analogy, the faith-instinct, oriented toward transcendence, self-sacrifice, and obedience, can be activated and misdirected on to substitute agents, who have a semblance of supernal authority and offer some species of "salvation." A conducive intellectual and cultural environment is an important factor for the proper "activation" of the faith-instinct. But false prophets indisputably exist; and if one's personal encounters are primarily with false prophets, can faith still operate constructively? Of course, even the worst charlatans can be catalysts to further exploration for "seekers," but social pressures, cultural norms, and dogmatic incrustations can offer formidable obstacles to such exploration. So it is important to be able to recognize true prophets, if they exist, and avoid the false ones. Do we have guidelines for this?

A thought experiment is in order: An extraordinary charismatic individual comes on the scene, claiming to have visions and revelations, with what seem to be lofty messages, and claiming to start a new religion or give a new direction and new life to an established religion. We hear his or her messages, and, along with others, face the choice

38. Seckler, 253.
39. Michael Buckley portrays the search for, and commitment to, truth as equivalent to belief in, and submission to, God. See *Denying and Disclosing God: The Ambiguous Progress of Modern Atheism* (New Haven, Conn.: Yale University Press, 2004), 133. For Aquinas, the openness to truth is just one aspect, albeit arguably the most important, of adherence to the natural law. For an extensive treatment of St. Thomas's teaching on natural law, see chap. 2 of my *Natural Law: an Introduction and Reexamination* (Chicago: Open Court, 2004).
40. See above, p. 103.

of placing faith in this person, or not. What should be our criterion? Should we look for miraculous signs? Or focus on personal morals, integrity, absence of personality disorders? Or check for consistency of the messages with prior revelations to which we have given credence in the past?

At the minimum, we might insist on the personal fidelity of the *prima-facie* divine messenger to the primary natural laws, as discussed above.[41] But obviously something more would be required to certify someone as a bona fide *prophet* send by God.

In the New Testament, Jesus offers some criteria to his disciples for avoiding false prophets:

> Beware of false prophets, who come to you in sheep's clothing, but underneath are ravenous wolves. By their fruits you will know them. Do people pick grapes from thorn bushes, or figs from thistles? Just so, every good tree bears good fruit, and a rotten tree bears bad fruit. A good tree cannot bear bad fruit, nor can a rotten tree bear good fruit.[42]

If we would ask for further clarification about how to discern which prophets fit into the category of "ravenous wolves" and/or what is the "bad fruit" that we should watch out for, the revered prophets of the Old Testament, dealing with the false prophets of their own milieu, go into considerable detail about who and what to look for: the *false* prophets characteristically lie about being sent by God;[43] they promote their own visions and predictions of the future;[44] they often plagiarize the ideas and expressions of true prophets in order to get credence from their hearers;[45] they are personally immoral, and condone immorality in their followers;[46] and/or they use religion greedily to increase their own wealth.[47]

Possibly the best modern example of plagiarizing by a reputed prophet is the creation of the Book of Mormon by Joseph Smith, the founder of the Church of Jesus Christ of Latter Day Saints (Mormons) in the nineteenth century. Smith claimed to receive golden plates at

---

41. On the significance of natural law in the choice of a religion, see my "Religious Commitment: The Natural-law Criteria," *Heythrop Journal* 50, no. 6, 2009.

42. Mt 7:15–18.

43. Is 23:32; Jer 14:14, 28:15.

44. Jer 23:16; Ez 13:2–4.

45. Is 23:30; Jer 23:30–31.

46. Is 23:17: Jer 23:14.

47. Ez 22:25.

the hands of the angel Moroni, from which he translated the Book of Mormon, with the help of two "seer stones," later called Urim and Thummin. The Book of Mormon on publication was replete with passages from the King James version of the Bible used at that time, including the mistranslations and misspellings that have been later discovered and corrected. These passages were used to develop a history of Hebrew tribes who, in spite of a complete lack of anthropological evidence, came to America under the leadership of Jesus Christ, after the Christian church founded by Jesus "apostatized" soon after the era of the Apostles.

Fantastically imaginative tales are another production of false prophets. Elijah Muhammad, the founder of the Nation of Islam, offers us an egregious example of this idiosyncratic creativity. According to Muhammad, blacks came into existence trillions of years ago, attained tremendous progress, but were obstructed by a mad black scientist, Mr. Yakub, who created the white race, the members of which would reign for six thousand years, until blacks finally regained their rightful place in the year 2000.

Unbridled sexual desires have been the hallmark of numerous "prophetic" personalities. Joseph Smith, advocating polygamy and promising eternal salvation to "celestial" wives who were married to him, took approximately forty-eight wives in addition to his first wife, Emma, who was often unaware of the other liaisons.[48] David Koresh, prophetic leader of the Branch Davidians, claimed that he was divinely entitled to sixty wives, but was joined to only twenty, including some teenagers, before the tragic assault of the FBI on the Waco headquarters of the sect in 1993. Elijah Muhammad had thirteen children by seven different mistresses, and also exemplified a lavish and greedy lifestyle, traveling around in a private jet, wearing a jeweled fez, and emptying the coffers of the Nation of Islam in prodigal gift-giving to his own family.

The personal characteristics and teachings of Muhammad, the prophet of Islam—if they had been known by the prophets of Israel—would have set off a series of "flashing red warning-lights." According to his eighth-century biographer, Ibn Ishaq, Muhammad participated in twenty-seven battles and thirty-eight raiding parties.[49] Various verses

48. See Brodie, *No Man Knows My History,* Appendix C.
49. See Muhammad Ishāq, *The Life of Muhammad,* trans. A. Guillaume (London: Oxford University Press, 1970), 659 ff.

in the Qur'an sanctified the taking of booty and slaves[50] and decreed that one-fifth of the booty should be given to himself for distribution as he saw fit.[51] Allowing his followers to have four wives, he received a divine exception to this rule,[52] and maintained a harem of fifteen wives, including a child-bride, Aisha; and Zaynab, the wife of his adopted son, Zayd, to whom he was attracted (Zayd, in response to Muhammad's perceived interest, divorced Zaynab, and Muhammad subsequently received special permission from Allah for the new arrangement).[53] Special permission was also granted by Allah for Muhammad's relationship with an Egyptian slave girl, Mary the Copt, after some of Muhammad's other wives had protested.[54] Lying, in order to avoid physical or mental injury, and to preserve the faith, is allowed to Muslims, according to the principle of *taqiyya* ("dissimulation");[55] and, according to the precedent of *Hudaybiyya* (named after a battle with that name), Muslims can break treaties with unbelievers, if and when they are strong enough to prevail against them.[56] The messages and patterns of behavior of Muhammad differ so radically from the guidelines given by the prophets of Israel that the traditional meanings of "prophet" and "prophecy" are completely abrogated.

But seduction by false prophets is not necessarily a dead-end road. In psychology and the social sciences, studies are sometimes conducted of "invulnerables"—underprivileged children or adolescents who have been raised in oppressive or abusive environments, and nevertheless not only survive but excel, thus challenging the predictive powers of social scientists who assess probable influences of environments. It is estimated that "invulnerables" are found in about 10 percent of such difficult situations. If the case of people of faith under the spell, or the jurisdiction, or the social pressures, of a false prophet, is somewhat analogous, we may speculate that an even higher percentage, *in spite of* all *prima-facie* obstacles to spiritual development from self-absorbed or perverted "prophets," can excel in implementing their faith. In pursuit of salvation, they can utilize the

50. Qur'an, Sura 8:41, 8:69.
51. Sura 8:41.
52. Sura 33:50.
53. Sura 33:37.
54. Sura 66:1–3.
55. Sura 2:22, 3:28, 5:89, 16:106.
56. Sura 2:217.

elements of spirituality and transcendence existing in every religion, and assiduously follow the dictates of conscience—that is, respecting life and the rights of others, furthering human and humane interests, and seeking truth at all costs. This is a well-worn ladder that has been available for seekers even under the influence of charlatans.

THE NECESSITY OF MIRACLES

Kenneth Woodward, in his analysis of miracles in the history of religions,[57] makes a distinction among various types of miracles and their significance. In the multiple branchings-out of Hinduism, miracles are taken as signs of spiritual power, as well as compassion for others. Miracles of Hindu gods like Krishna and holy men like Shankara and the "poet saints" consist of curing sicknesses and raising the dead. In yoga, as the ascetical/mystical offshoot of Hinduism, high states of perfection became associated with miraculous powers such as superhuman strength and the ability to levitate and traverse great distances in a moment's time. Buddhism disavows the importance of miracles, but many miracles were purportedly associated with the birth, life and death of Gautama Buddha. And Buddhist holy men reportedly have acquired a variety of psychic and psychokinetic powers. In Islam, following the example of Muhammad, no official importance is placed on miracles, although legends exist of holy Muslims curing sicknesses, walking on water, etc. But in the Hebrew Bible and the New Testament, miracles are ways for God to give His stamp of approval and support for the messages conveyed by Moses, the prophets, Jesus, and the missionaries of early Christianity.

Thus, although Jesus complains that "unless you people see signs and wonders, you will not believe,"[58] and the resurrected Jesus mildly chides Thomas the Apostle for demanding to inspect his wounds, saying "Blessed are those who have not seen and have believed,"[59] nevertheless he exhorts the doubters, "Believe me that I am in the Father and the Father is in me, or else, believe because of the works themselves," and "Even if you do not believe in me, believe the works."[60]

---

57. See Kenneth L. Woodward, *The Book of Miracles: The Meaning of the Miracle Stories in Christianity, Judaism, Buddhism and Islam* (New York: Simon & Schuster, 2000).

58. Jn 4:48

59. Jn 20:29.

60. Jn 10:38, 14:11.

And in sending out his disciples to preach the Gospel, he promises an extraordinary amount of supernatural authentication: "In my name they will drive out demons, they will speak new languages. They will pick up serpents, and if they drink any deadly thing, it will not harm them. They will lay hands on the sick, and they will recover."[61] The Acts of the Apostles accordingly report numerous healings,[62] a resuscitation from the dead,[63] and multiple miraculous rescues from prison[64] as signs of God's providential support of the apostolic initiatives.

But these developments are long ago and far away. Should we expect any continuation of such miraculous support for the Gospel message? Or are people now any less prone to require concrete signs of authentication than in the early days of Christianity? Do "doubting Thomases" deserve any special divine help in our own era? For some who are not "blessed for believing without having seen," it would seem that something miraculous would almost be necessary to make possible the leap from unbelief to faith.

Protestants differ about the possibility and/or the importance of miracles in our day—ranging from the belief of some Evangelicals in miraculous healings and conversions, to the skepticism of many Protestants about miracles as a leftover "Romish" focus on the sensory and the sensational, in lieu of true biblically inspired faith.

Catholic tradition is more sanguine. Pope St. Pius X in a *motu proprio* in 1910 declared that miracles are "most certain signs of the divine origin of the Christian religion." Claims of the miraculous are taken into account by Catholicism, and sometimes recognized, although rational and even skeptical inquiry is a prerequisite in dealing with such claims. For example, before the canonization of a saint, miracles are required, and medical examiners, along with other experts and a "devil's advocate," are appointed to rule out possible natural explanations of the alleged miraculous development. At the shrine of Lourdes in France, a permanent medical office that has access to medical specialists conducts meticulous examination of cures, and conveys a final decision to ecclesiastical authorities.

During the twentieth century, the most renowned *public* Christian miracles include the "miracle of the sun" witnessed by sixty thousand people in Fatima, Portugal, at noon on Oct. 13, 1917. The exact date

61. Mk 16:17–18.
62. Acts 3:4, 5:15–16, 28:8–9.
63. Acts 20:9.
64. Acts 5:19, 12:7, 16:26.

and time of this miracle, which coincided with the Russian "October Revolution," was predicted months previously by the Virgin Mary appearing to three peasant children.[65] Lucia, one of the children, mentioned that the Virgin told her an even greater miracle could have been performed if there had not been such a lack of faith (manifested by skeptics who harassed the children and even jailed them). Major public modern signs also include the miracles at Soufanieh in Damascus, Syria, dedicated to the promotion of Christian unity and including miraculous copious exudations of olive oil, and the stigmata of the crucifixion appearing on the body of Myrna Nazzour whenever the dates for Roman Catholic and Orthodox celebrations of Easter coincide;[66] and also the multiple silent apparitions, documented by some photographs and videos, of the Virgin Mary in Zeitun, Egypt, during 1968 and 1969, witnessed by tens of thousands of Christians and Muslims, reported by Egyptian news media, and investigated by government authorities as well as religious officials.[67]

It goes without saying, however, that there is an ever-present danger that people with an appetite for sensationalism may hanker after the miraculous for its own sake. In this case, the desire to satisfy avid curiosity could be detrimental to faith. Thus Jesus, when the scribes and Pharisees asked him to show them a sign from heaven, characterized them as a "wicked and adulterous generation, and refused their request;[68] and, in one of his parables, Jesus depicts Abraham saying someone who has not listened to Moses and the prophets would not reform their lives—even if someone in hell were to appear before them miraculously and warn them.[69] Contemporary reports of claims of supernatural visions, sometimes with messages, are no doubt often meant to accommodate the sort of prurient curiosity that Jesus warned against. Randall Sullivan, a contributing editor of *Rolling Stone* magazine, decided to do detective work investigating such claims.[70] The book that resulted covers numerous cases in 450 pages, but spends the most time in interviews and investigations in

65. See Stanley Jaki, *God and the Sun at Fatima* (Royal Oak, Mich.: Real View Books, 1999).

66. See Elias Zahlaoui, *Soufanieh: Chronique des apparitions et manifestations de Jesus et de Marie, a Damas*, 1982–1990 (Paris: O.E.I.L., 1991).

67. See Pearl Zaki, *Before Our Eyes: The Virgin Mary, Zeitun, Egypt 1968 and 1969* (Goleta, Calif.: Queenship Pub., 2002).

68. Mt 16:4.

69. Lk 16:24.

70. See *The Miracle Detective: An Investigation of Holy Visions* (New York: Atlantic Monthly Press, 2004).

Medjugorje, in Bosnia Herzegovina, where six young people claimed to have received visions and messages from the Virgin Mary in 1981. The claims of the six seers have continued since that time, resulting in a total of over thirty-five thousand alleged visions or messages, although all the bishops in charge of Medjugorje have refused ecclesiastical recognition, and have even strongly characterized the phenomenon as "non-supernatural."[71] Pilgrims to Medjugorje claim to witness miracles such as their Rosary chains turning a gold color or spectacles of the sun whirling in the sky. The journal *The Skeptical Inquirer*, which specializes in debunking bogus miracle claims, has published critical analyses of Medjugorje and other phenomena, but no in-depth analysis of the three public miracles mentioned above.

The philosopher Søren Kierkegaard, in staunch Lutheran fashion distrustful of miracles, declared that faith itself is a miracle, or better —is *the* miracle, the great miracle of subjectivity performed by God.[72] Kierkegaard apparently was motivated to this viewpoint by a misunderstanding of Hume's treatise on miracles,[73] where Hume concludes that, since miracles are completely contrary to the laws of nature, and thus irrational, faith would indeed be the greatest miracle of all! In view of Hume's inveterate and unceasing skepticism, this "conclusion" is obviously meant ironically. It is possible, of course, that a conversion experience, although intensely personal and private, could be a springboard to faith. But not every conversion experience is clearly miraculous, like the sudden conversion of St. Paul described in the Acts of the Apostles,[74] or Augustine's sudden and absolute conversion described in his autobiography.[75]

The faith of an individual may or may not be catalyzed by an external or "subjective" miracle. But the *necessity* of miracles is most evident in cases where competing religions are claiming to have divine authorization. One who is making a choice between competing claims is not unreasonable in demanding an official "signature." To

---

71. See my 2006 Marquette University Aquinas Lecture, *Five Metaphysical Paradoxes* (Milwaukee, Wis.: Marquette University Press, 2006), 44.

72. See *Fear and Trembling,* trans. Walter Lowrie (Princeton, NJ: Princeton University Press, 1974), 47, 52, 77.

73. *An Enquiry Concerning Human Understanding,* sect. 10, pt. 2, §101. Kierkegaard read this interpretation in the writings of Johann Georg Hamman, possibly without knowing that Hume was the author. See Louis Pojman, "Christianity and Philosophy in Kierkegaard's Early Papers," *Journal of the History of Ideas* 44, no. 1 (1983): 135.

74. Acts 9:4, 22:8.

75. Aurelius Augustine, *Confessions* VIII, 29.

commit oneself unreservedly to a supposedly supernatural religion that has shown no clear signs of divine approval is like signing a contract without expecting, or even requiring, a countersigner.

PUTTING ONESELF IN THE SHOES OF ATHEISTS

What is going on in the mind of an atheist when confronted with the idea of God and the fact that, for numerous believers, God is not just an idea but a concrete reality? Formidable and seemingly insuperable obstacles to faith stand in the way of the unbeliever. What he or she usually perceives in persons of faith is a strange gravitation to nothing less than *adult fairy tales*. Some believers extol a God who evolved from a previous human state; some look forward in anticipation to an afterlife filled with sensuous delights, eating and drinking and unceasing erotic episodes (even with perpetual procreation of gods and goddesses to populate the planets of the universe); some preach the possibility of reincarnation after reincarnation in the pursuit of some final exquisite perfection. But the most egregious fairy tale of all seems to be the belief of some that the Creator of the universe made humans in His own image, sent His Son to take on flesh, and is preparing eternal happiness for each of His adopted sons and daughters.

The implications of this latter belief boggle the imagination. Are we really to believe that God created the universe with the trillions of galaxies in the macrocosm and the exquisite architecture of the atomic and subatomic realm, with humans in mind? That He is not only aware of every sparrow that falls[76] to the ground, and clothes the lilies of the field with conscientious care,[77] but also numbers the hairs of each individual[78] and provides each with everything required for their eternal salvation? That the Son of God would have really decided to enter into the womb of a woman in order to become incarnate? That He would want to become subject to all that humans experience—not just the sufferings, but the indignities and humiliations of ordinary life—hunger and thirst, fatigue, elimination, sweating, uncertainties (possibly after a suspension of divine foreknowledge)? That he would be willing to sacrifice himself for all the billions of people

76. Mt 10:29.
77. Lk 12:27.
78. Lk 12:7.

who have inhabited the earth and are living now? And—not the least important factor—that He would predestine all humans after death for a restoration of the body and the possibility of seeing God, in a kingdom where death would be a thing of the past? If a Christian realizes the enormity of what he himself believes in ("Good News" is an understatement), he should have nothing but empathy for the hesitance of the atheist to open his mind to faith.

On the other hand, for a person of faith whose mind is hardwired to look for *causes*, the notion that we and our universe or multiple universes simply emerged out of nothing by an infinite number of chance developments seems to be an incomparably incredible fairy tale, a threat to rationality itself.

Bibliography

Aquinas, Thomas, *Opera omnia*. Leonine edition. Rome, 1972.

———. *In IV libros Sententiarum Commentaria, ex manuscriptis bibliothecae Tolosanae conuentus Sancti Thomae Aquinatis*. Tolosae, Apus Colomerium, 1649–1652. Ridgewood, N.J.: Gregg Press, 1964.

———. *Sancti Thomae Aquinatis Tractatus de Substantiis Separatis*. Edited by Francis Lescoe. West Hartford: St. Joseph College, 1962.

———. *Summa contra gentiles*. Rome: Desclée & C.–Herder, 1934.

———. *Summa theologiae*. Five volumes. Madrid: Biblioteca de Autores Cristianos, 1958.

Aristotle. *The Basic Works of Aristotle*. Edited by Richard McKeon. New York: Random House, 1941.

Augustine, Aurelius. *Confessions*. Translated by Maria Boulding. New York: Vintage, 1998.

Barbour, Ian. *Nature, Human Nature, and God*. Minneapolis: Fortress, 2002.

Barrow, John D., and Frank J. Tipler. *The Anthropic Cosmological Principle*. Oxford: Oxford University Press, 1986.

Barth, Karl. *Church Dogmatics*. Translated by G. T. Thomson. Edinburg: T. & T. Clark, 1936–77.

Beauvoir, Simone de. *Adieu: A Farewell to Sartre*. Translated by Patrick O'Brian, New York: Pantheon, 1984.

Behe, Michael. *Darwin's Black Box: The Biochemical Challenge to Evolution*. New York: Free Press, 1996.

———. *The Edge of Evolution: The Search for the Limits of Darwinism*. New York: Free Press, 2007.

Berlinski, David. *The Devil's Delusion: Atheism and Its Scientific Pretensions*. New York: Crown Forum, 2008.

Blumenthal, David R. *The Commentary of R. Hoter ben Shelomo to the Thirteen Principles of Maimonides*. Leiden: E. J. Brill, 1974.

Brodie, Fawn. *No Man Knows My History: The Life of Joseph Smith, the Mormon Prophet*. New York: Alfred Knopf, 1971.

Brown, Raymond, Joseph Fitzmyer, and Roland Murphy, eds., *The New Jerome Biblical Commentary*. Englewood Cliffs, N.J.: Prentice Hall, 1968.

Buckley, Michael J., S.J. *Denying and Disclosing God: The Ambiguous Progress of Modern Atheism.* New Haven: Yale University Press, 2004.

Collins, Francis. *The Language of God: A Scientist Presents Evidence for Belief.* New York: Free Press, 2006.

D'Aquili, Eugene G, and Andrew B. Newberg, *The Mystical Mind: Probing the Biology of Religious Experience.* Minneapolis: Fortress Press, 1999.

———. *Why God Won't Go Away.* New York: Ballantine, 2001.

Darwin, Charles. *Works of Charles Darwin.* Edited by Paul H. Barrett and R. B. Freeman. Charlottesville, Va.: Intelex Corporation, 2001.

Dashti, 'Ali, *Twenty Three Years: A Study of the Prophetic Career of Mohammad.* Translated by F. R. C. Bagley. London: George Allen & Unwin, 1985.

Davies, Paul. *The Cosmic Blueprint: New Discoveries in Nature's Creative Ability to Order the Universe.* New York: Simon and Schuster, 1988.

———. *God and the New Physics.* New York: Simon and Schuster, 1983.

Dawkins, Richard. *The God Illusion.* Boston: Houghton Mifflin Co., 2006.

Dembski, William, ed. *Mere Creation: Science, Faith & Intelligent Design.* Downers Grove, Ill.: InterVarsity Press, 1998.

———. "Why Evolutionary Algorithms Cannot Generate Specified Complexity." *Metaviews* 152.

Denton, Michael. *Evolution: A Theory in Crisis.* Bethesda, Md.: Adler & Adler, 1986.

Doctrine and Covenants of the Church of Jesus Christ of Latter-day Saints. Salt Lake, Utah: Church of Jesus Christ of Latter-Day Saints, 1982.

Drey, Johann Sebastian. *Brief Introduction to the Study of Theology.* Translated by Michael J. Himes. Notre Dame, Ind.: University of Notre Dame Press, 1994.

Epictetus, *The Golden Sayings of Epictetus.* Translated by Hastings Crossley. Harvard Classics Edition. New York: P. F. Collier & Sons, 1937.

Flew, Antony, *God and Philosophy.* Amherst, New York: Prometheus Books, 2005.

———, with Roy Abraham Varghese. *There Is a God: How the World's Most Notorious Atheist Changed His Mind.* New York: Harper One, 2007.

Freud, Sigmund. *The Ego and the Id.* Riviere transl. New York: Norton, 1962.

Hart, David Bentley. *The Doors of the Sea: Where Was God in the Tsunami?* Grand Rapids, Mich.: William B. Eerdmans, 2005.

Hart, Hendrik, Johan van der Hoeven, and Nicholas Wolterstorff, eds. *Rationality in the Calvinian Tradition.* Lanham, Md,: University Press of America, 1983.

Hartshorne, Charles. *Omnipotence and Other Theological Mistakes.* Albany: State University of New York, 1984.

Hegel, G. W. F. *Phenomenology of Mind.* Baillie transl. New York: Harper Torchbooks, 1967.

Hoyle, Fred. "The Universe: Past and Present Reflections." *Annual Reviews of Astronomy and Astrophysics* 20 (1982).

Hume, David. *Dialogues Concerning Natural Religion* X. Indianapolis: Bobbs-Merrill, 1981.

Hunter, Cornelius. *Darwin's God: Evolution and the Problem of Evil.* Grand Rapids, Mich.: Brazos Press, 2001.

———. *Science's Blind Spot: The Unseen Religion of Scientific Naturalism.* Grand Rapids, Mich.: Brazos Press, 2007.

Huxley, Aldous. *The Perennial Philosophy.* New York: Harper Colophon Books, 1945.

Ishāq, Muhammad. *The Life of Muhammad.* Translated by A. Guillaume. London: Oxford University Press, 1970.

Jaki, Stanley. *God and the Sun at Fatima.* Royal Oak, Mich.: Real View Books, 1999.

———. *The Purpose of It All.* Washington, D. C.: Regnery Gateway, 1990.

———. *Questions on Science and Religion.* Port Huron, Mich.: Real View Books, 2004.

Kainz, Howard P. *"Active and Passive Potency" in Thomistic Angelology.* The Hague: Nijoff, 1972.

———. *Democracy and the "Kingdom of God."* Dordrecht and Milwaukee: Kluwer and Marquette University Press, 1993.

———. *Ethics in Context.* Washington, D. C.: Georgetown University Press, 1988.

———. *Natural Law: An Introduction and Reexamination.* Chicago: Open Court, 2004.

———. *Philosophy of Human Nature.* Chicago: Open Court, 2008.

Kierkegaard, Søren. *Concluding Unscientific Postscript.* Swenson transl. Princeton: Princeton University Press, 1941.

———. *Either/Or.* Translated by Walter Lowrie. New York: Anchor, 1959.

Leibniz, Gottfried Wilhelm, *Theodicy: Essays on the Goodness of God, the Freedom of Man, and the Origin of Evil.* Translated by E. M. Huggard. New Haven: Yale University Press, 1952.

Levenson, Jon. *Resurrection and the Restoration of Israel: The Ultimate Victory of the God of Life.* New Haven: Yale University Press, 2006.

———. and Kevin Manning. *Resurrection: The Power of God for Christians and Jews.* New Haven: Yale University Press, 2008.

Lewis, C. S. *Mere Christianity.* New York: Macmillan, 1952.

Lubac, Henri de. *The Mystery of the Supernatural.* New York: Herder & Herder, 1967.

Luther, Martin. *Sermons of Martin Luther: The Church Postils.* Translated by Eugene Klug et al. Grand Rapids, Mich.: Baker Books, 1996.

Maimonides, Moses. *Guide of the Perplexed.* 2d ed. Translated by M. Friedlander. New York: Dover Publications, 1956.

Mascaró, Juan. transl. *The Upanishads.* Baltimore: Penguin Books, 1973.

Meyer, Stephen C., "DNA and Other Designs." *First Things* 102, April 2000, 30–38.

———. *Signature in the Cell: DNA and the Evidence for Intelligent Design.* New York: Harper One, 2009.

———. "Intelligent Design: The Origin of Biological Information and the Higher Taxonomic Categories." *Proceedings of the Biological Society of Washington* (117:2, 2004): 213–39.

New American Bible, The. Wichita, Kans.: Devore & Sons, 1987.

Noll, Mark, and Carolyn Nystrom. *Is the Reformation Over?* Grand Rapids, Mich.: Baker Academic, 2005.

Pastore, Nicholas. *The Nature-Nurture Controversy.* New York: King's Crown Press, 1949.

Pickthall, Mohammed Marmaduke, transl. *The Glorious Qur'an,* Elmhurst, N.Y.: Tahrike Tarsile Qur'an, Inc., 2000.

Pinker, Stephen. *The Blank Slate: The Modern Denial of Human Nature.* New York: Viking, 2003.

Plato. *The Dialogues of Plato.* Translated by Bede Jowett. Two volumes. New York: Random House, 1937.

Rahner, Karl. *Theological Investigations.* Translated by David Bourke. London: Darton, Longman & Todd, 1976.

Ross, Hugh. *The Creator and the Cosmos.* Colorado Springs: Navpress, 2001.

Sanford, J. C. *Genetic Entropy & the Mystery of the Genome.* Lima, New York: Elim Publishing, 2005.

Sarna, Nahum, *Exodus, The Traditional Hebrew Text with the New JPS Translation.* New York: Jewish Publication Society, 1991.

Sartre, Jean-Paul. *The Words.* Translated by Bernard Frechtman. New York: Braziller, 1964.

Schönborn, Christoph Cardinal, *Chance or Purpose?: Creation, Evolution, and a Rational Faith.* Translated by Henry Taylor. San Francisco: Ignatius Press, 2007.

Seckler, Max. *Instinkt und Glaubenswille nach Thomas von Aquin.* Mainz: Matthias-Grünewald-Verlag, 1961.

———. "Potentia oboedientialis bei Karl Rahner (1904–1984) und Henri de Lubac (1896–1991)," *Gregorianum* 78, no. 4, 1997.

Simmons, Geoffrey. *Billions of Missing Links.* Eugene, Oreg.: Harvest House, 2007.

Smith, Joseph. *Teachings of the Prophet Joseph Smith.* Salt Lake: Deseret News Press, 1938.

Steele, David Ramsay. *Atheism Explained.* Chicago: Open Court, 2008.

Stove, David. *Darwinian Fairytales.* Brookfield, Vt.: Avebury/Ashgate, 1995.

Sullivan, Randall. *The Miracle Detective: An Investigation of Holy Visions.* New York: Atlantic Monthly Press, 2004.

Teilhard de Chardin, Pierre. *Human Energy.* Translated by J. M. Cohen. New York: Harcourt Brace Jovanovich, 1962.

———. *The Human Phenomenon.* Translated by Sarah Appleton-Weber. Portland, Oreg.: Sussex Academic Press, 1999.

Thaxton, Charles, Walter Bradley, and Roger Olsen. *The Mystery of Life's Origin: Reassessing Current Theories.* New York: Philosophical Library, 1984.

Tipler, Frank. *The Physics of Christianity.* New York: Doubleday, 2007.

Unamuno, Miguel de. *Tragic Sense of Life.* New York: Dover Publications, 1954.

Voltaire, Francois Marie Arouet de, *Toleration and Other Essays.* Translated, with an Introduction, by Joseph McCabe. New York: G. P. Putnam's Sons, 1912.

Weigel, George. *Faith, Reason, and the War against Jihadism*. New York: Doubleday, 2007.

Wheelwright, Philip, ed. *The Presocratics*. New York: Odyssey Press, 1966.

Woodward, Kenneth L. *The Book of Miracles: The Meaning of the Miracle Stories in Christianity, Judaism, Buddhism and Islam*. New York: Simon & Schuster, 2000.

Yogananda, Paramahansa, *Autobiography of a Yogi*. London: Rider & Co., 1969.

Index